drink

SUSY ATKINS AND DAVE BROOM

Dedication To Boris, Anna, Clara, Daniel & Charlie, the drinkers of the future.

Drink

By Susy Atkins and Dave Broom
Published in the USA by
Willow Creek Press
PO Box 147, Minocqua, WI 54548

ISBN: 1 57223-406-7

UK edition ISBN: 1-84000-350-2

First published in Great Britain in 2001 by
Mitchell Beazley, an imprint of Octopus Publishing
Group Limited, 2–4 Heron Quays, London E14 4JP.

The author and publishers will be grateful for any information which will assist them in keeping
future editions up to date. Although all reasonable care has been taken in the preparation of
this book, neither the publishers nor the author can accept any liability for any consequences
arising from the use thereof, or the information contained therein.

Commissioning Editor Rebecca Spry
Executive Art Editors Phil Ormerod, Tracy Killick
Managing Editors Hilary Lumsden, Jamie Grafton
Design Colin Goody
Editor Susan Keevil
Photography Russell Sadur
Production Nancy Roberts
Index Mary Kirkness

Typeset in Rotis Semi Sans Serif
Printed and bound by Toppan Printing Company in China

Acknowledgements
Dave and Susy would like to thank: Steven Morris, Paul Henry, Enotria Winecellars,
Anne Whitehurst, German Wine Information Service,Catherine Manac'h, SOPEXA,Victoria Morrall,
Wines of Austria,Ted Bruning, CAMRA, Salvo Alfano, Cactus Blue restaurant, R&R Teamwork,
Virgin Wines (pics), Michael Jackson, Jim Beveridge, Neil Cochrane, Nick Morgan, Mike Nicolson,
UDV, Vanya Cullen,Henry Butler (for his palate), Viv Stanshall, Bruce Fraser, for cosmic particle
theory, Jo and Ian, for great ideas at times of crisis, and the Havana crew
Thanks also to Becca, Colin, Jamie, Susan, and the ever-lovely Hils.

The authors and staff at Mitchell Beazley would like to thank Unwins and Debbie Collinson for their kind
help in supplying drinks for the special photography in this book. We would also like to thank Martin
Turner at Riedel UK for glasses, Liebherr for the fridge and Glenfiddich for the germinating grains.

Contents

Apéritif

'If I had all the money I'd spent on drink, I'd spend it on drink.' The sentiment of Viv Stanshall's greatest creation, Sir Henry Rawlinson, is one with which we heartily concur, though perhaps, unlike Sir Henry, we'd make sure we were buying decent gear. Never has the consumer been so spoiled for choice when it comes to the range and quality of alcohol on offer, and never have so many people been interested not only in wine, but in beer and spirits too; yet never has it been so problematic to decide what to buy. There's still a great deal of rough and boring booze out there, sitting on the shelf alongside terrific bargains. Increased choice doesn't always make for an easier purchase...

It's no surprise that people end up buying the same thing week in week out. We've spoken to friends who have said 'I really hate that oaky Chardonnay' while holding a bottle of...you guessed it, oaky Chardonnay (usually a white Burgundy, which they think is made from another grape entirely). Why did they buy the same style of wine? Because no-one had taken the time to give them basic information on what the alternatives were. That's what this book is trying to do. We realized that while there was a mass of excellent books about wines, spirits and beers out there for the connoisseur, there wasn't one which talked to those of you who liked a drink and wanted to know more about the topic without becoming a Master of Wine, or a Guru of Gin. If you are itching to know the precise details of the soil content in Puligny-Montrachet, or the history of the Mondavi family, then buy another book (actually, we harbor a sneaking desire that this guide should inspire you to dig deeper for knowledge in specific fields). For now, though, it's useful to know about the main grape varieties and styles of wine you are liable to bump up against in the bottle shop or restaurant. Here each grape gets its own entry along with an idea of how it performs around the world. We tell you what it should taste like at its best, and when to avoid it. There's also a section on some of the 'also-ran' grapes which are less commonly seen but which we believe deserve their 15 minutes (or more) of fame or need debunking. The same goes for the different styles of fortified wines, sparklers, spirits and beers.

We don't apologise for being opinionated. What's the point of assuming that everything is great! fantastic! brilliant! when it palpably isn't? Once you've started tasting wine, beer and spirits in a more informed way, you might not agree with everything we say about the flavors and aromas (or the quality) of some drinks. Good! We just want you to have an idea of what you are being offered so that when you try it you'll know more about what you like. And then we vehemently hope you will enjoy your chosen bottles and have fun drinking them. Ah yes, fun. Remember that? You'd be forgiven for thinking that the whole subject of alcoholic drink has to be approached in a deeply reverential fashion. Pants to that, we say.

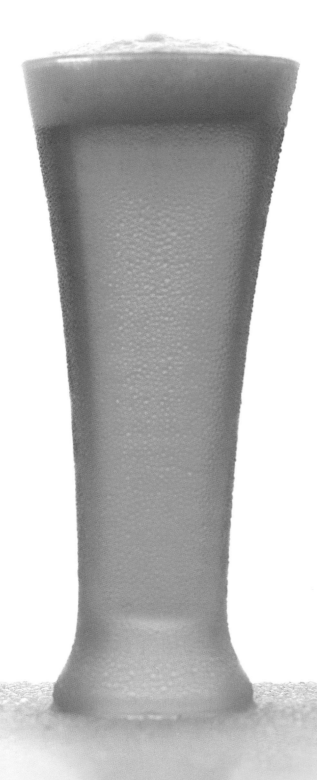

Forget the PC attitude of many drinks books. Drink is meant to be fun. There is a mass of information out there, all of which is fascinating to a greater or lesser degree, but at the end of the day when you pull the cork on a bottle of wine, take a sip of beer or a slug of whisky you are doing so because you want to enjoy yourself.

Drink is for the good times, not for pontificating over. So, talking of good times, we've included a section on parties and party drinks, a chapter on cocktails (including some dead-easy ones) and a short summary of food-and-wine matching made simple. One thing is for sure: you won't like some of the styles we recommend. No-one likes everything (thank God). All we ask is that you give different drinks a chance. That's why, at the end of each chapter, we've given you a 'flavor' or 'family tree' showing how various types of drink are related to each other. There's a good chance that if you like 'X' then you may like 'Y' from the same tree. Give it a shot! As for education, we pray for the day when every liquor store and supermarket starts educating their staff so they can give informed advice. We long for waiting staff in bars and restaurants to be taught which wine goes with which dish, what beer or spirit is the right one for the occasion. It's not difficult, it's not expensive and it benefits the customer, the staff and the business. Until that day dawns you might as well get as much information as you can. Happy drinking!

Exploding myths

Gloves off! There's so much guff, pish and general baloney spoken about drink that it often seems as if you need a degree in 'appreciation' to be able to understand it. There is such a mass of contradictory advice handed down from on high by so-called 'experts' that it's no great surprise that your knees go to jelly when confronted with 300 bottles of wine in a shop, or a bar filled with hundreds of spirits. Our first bit of advice is steer clear of self-professed wine-buffs, whose knowledge is often limited and riddled with snobbery. This book is about getting realistic about drink, so to kick things off, here are some of the more common myths that surround it, and the reasons why they need to be exploded.

MYTH *Red wines should be served warm.* Don't put that bottle by the fire, near the boiler or under grandma's buttocks. Warm red wine is a real no-no, and tastes stewed and jammy, or just oddly muted in character. Rich reds are best served at room temperature (or even a shade cooler), while soft, juicy reds actually benefit from a very light chill to bring out their tangy fruit flavours. Many restaurants still don't get it: demand a cooler bottle or an ice bucket if served blackcurrant jam. While we're on the subject, don't chill whites too hard – unless they are particularly vile, in which case, chill them into oblivion.

MYTH *New World wines taste completely different to Old World wines.* It was once the case that anyone could differentiate between a classic Aussie wine (rich and ultra-fruity) and a classic French one (elegant and restrained or rough and rustic). It was all to do with the New World's obsession with new technology (producing squeaky clean, laboratory-concocted Stepford Wines) versus the European belief in *terroir* (the flavours and aromas conjured up by a particular plot of land, its climate, and with minimal human intervention). Now the irony is that many Europeans are embracing the high-tech approach, and the rest are trying to establish a stronger sense of *terroir*. The lines have blurred, and wines are getting better as this exchange of information increases.

MYTH *You must let fine red wine 'breathe' by removing the cork an hour or so before drinking.* Rubbish. Hardly any wine is in contact with air while it is still in the bottle. If you want your wine to open up and mellow out, man, pour it into a decanter or jug to aerate it properly, or simply swirl it round vigorously in big glasses at the table.

MYTH *Corked wine refers to little pieces of cork floating around in the liquid.* No, that's crap-cork wine, and the flotsam certainly doesn't make any difference to the flavor. Corked flavors and aromas (think of the smell of musty, damp cardboard) occur because a chemical (known as TCA) produced by the cork taints the wine. We estimate that around 5 percent of all wine is affected. Meanwhile, bear in mind that plastic stoppers never produce cork taint.

MYTH *Blends are inferior to single varietal wines.* Just because your wine says Cabernet Sauvignon on the label, instead of Cab-Shiraz, doesn't necessarily make it a better wine. Some varieties are much better in pairs, or trios. More complexity and depth of flavor can be achieved by blending them cleverly with suitable partners. Most of the greatest clarets are blends. There are bad blends and bad varietals, but varietals seem to be fashionable now. And not all single malt whiskies (the product of one distillery) are better than all blended whiskies. Same principle.

MYTH *The sommelier (wine waiter) is always right.* Absolutely wrong. YOU are always right, so ask for advice, but then pick the wine YOU want, and if it is disappointing, send it straight back. The so-called experts of the wine trade may know a bit about the subject, but they do not know what YOU like! It's time to take control! Read on...

White wine

Knock back a glass of wine without the **liquid** touching the sides and you're missing out big time. That's not to suggest hours of **drooling** and cooing over each mouthful – especially in public. But just a moment or two thinking about the **aromas** and flavors will pay off. You'll enjoy fine wine all the more, and you will learn which styles of wine suit you best and – crucially – you'll be able to spot an absolute **bummer** at first sniff.

Chill, swirl, sniff, slurp and swallow

Here's how to taste white wine like a pro. Chill your bottle ever-so lightly – frosty white tends to have a muted character, so the aromas stay hidden. Use a clear, plain glass, and pour out a small measure: enough to enable you to swirl the liquid without slopping it everywhere.

Do looks really matter?

Now take a good look – a very pale color indicates a light, dry, unoaked white, while a deeper yellow implies a richer style, possibly oaked, maybe sweeter. The wine should be clear, not cloudy. Little white crystals look odd, but are harmless tartrate deposits which won't affect the flavor. Look at texture too – is it thick and unctuous (high alcohol or sweetness) or thin and light? Then swish the wine around the glass to release more aroma and take a huge sniff...

Getting nosy with it

...Or a series of small sniffs, which some experts find more effective as it doesn't overload the nostrils. While you do it, decide whether the wine smells fresh, sulphurous or musty. If the aroma is attractive, then why? For example, is it fruity (if so, which fruits can you smell?), floral, buttery or oaky? Most of the time we don't pay enough attention to the perfume of a wine, but it provides an important part of the sensory thrill and can tell you a lot about the overall character of the liquid you are about to drink, so take your time. Sniff away!

A waste of taste...?

Now take a big slurp and, rather than simply swallowing, swill the wine around your mouth, perhaps drawing a little air into it to release the flavors further. Think about the style of the wine – its sweetness or dryness, its level of acidity and its texture (how rich and viscous is it?). You might also spot specific flavors at this point – white wine tasters routinely find citrus or tropical fruits, hints of grass or leaf, butter and cream, a mineral note and even white pepper. Or you might find something quite different. Don't worry about this for a second. If you think your white tastes of caramel-dipped popcorn or banana chews, then fine. It's what it means to YOU that counts, not whether you've impressed a stuck-up wine waiter. After you've swallowed the wine (or spat it out) try to decide whether the flavor lingered in your mouth or disappeared abruptly. That's what we in the trade call the 'finish' – short or long.

Think pink

In a rosé, look carefully at the color (this'll be anything from the palest baby pink to tomato red), then expect red berry flavors, tangy acidity, or perhaps some sweetness. Many rosés are disappointingly flabby – they lack the crispness to keep them balanced – so be aware of the freshness of your pink wine.

Do I have to wear an anorak?

If you're really serious about wine tasting, then whatever is in your glass, make a few notes. They don't have to be long-winded. It's amazing how quickly a few well-chosen words will help you recall the flavors of a particularly delicious wine, or a truly disgusting one.

Chardonnay

Had enough Ch... you know what?

Fair enough – some drinkers are bored with Chardonnay. It crops up all over the winemaking globe and when it's made in the very richly oaked style, it can quickly get tiresome. But if you're sick of this sort of Chardonnay, it's quite possibly not the grape variety itself you dislike, but the over-zealous use of toasted oak.

But it's taking over the world!

Look at it this way. A winemaker wants as little hassle as possible. Ideally, he's after a compliant grape, one that behaves itself in the vineyard and the winery, doing his bidding without so much as a growl. One that will bounce up to new consumers like a loveable Labrador puppy – soft, golden and cuddly. That's Chardonnay for you. It's a winemaker's grape. No matter what he wants to do, Chardonnay just rolls over and lets him get on with it. He can craft it in a whistle-clean and bone dry style, or turn it out generously fleshy and peachy, or perhaps render it toasty and spicy with heavy vanilla-oak character.

A case of Chard-U-like?

Of course. Ironically, Chardonnay has become shorthand for oaky, fruity, soft and undemanding white wine, just when winemakers are trying to give it more elegance. Inevitably for a grape that is grown everywhere, there is an ocean of blandly boring wine around but, equally, there is a wide range of fascinating styles. Naked Chardonnay, with no oak-ageing, can be nervy and pure, tasting of apples and lemons. Look to cooler climates for this racier, crisper style. Even oaked Chardonnay ranges from the buttered fruit salad wines of warmer spots to elaborate concoctions with nuts and honeysuckle to the fore.

How much then?

Today there are simple, gluggable, cheap Chardonnays (from Eastern Europe, say); bright, sunny, judiciously oaked New World wines in the mid-price bracket (Chile, Australia and the Languedoc); and deeply complex, great wines (white burgundies, top Californians...) that it's better to try when someone else is paying. And there are bubbles: Chardonnay is one of the grapes behind Champagne and many other top sparkling wines. A versatile beast, all in all.

And Chardonnay blends?

Hmm. There are half-decent blends with Sauvignon, Chenin or Colombard and it is very successfully blended with Pinot Noir in fizz, but as table wine we'd rather drink it on its own.

CELLAR, GLASS & PLATE

Storing: Light, unoaked Chardonnays need drinking up quickly, as do the softly oaked, commercial ones. Richer, more complex, oaky wines will last a decade or more. Although we prefer crisp fresh acidity in ours, and drink them earlier, nutty, mellow white burgundy at 15 years plus is a big turn-on for others.

Serving: Always serve chilled.

Food matching: Chardonnay is extremely food-friendly. Serve a light wine with simple shellfish, and crack open a riper, richer one with roast poultry, rich seafood (salmon, crab or lobster), or fish in a buttery sauce.

More worldwide hits than Elvis

Argentina

Chardonnay features large in Argentina's bid to become an international player. Some impressive wines have appeared, but so far they are squeaky clean, with little to say that's distinctive. New vineyards in the high-altitude Tupungato region could provide more excitement.

Australia

The home of modern-day Chardonnay. In its earliest incarnation Aussie Chardonnay was about as OTT as a wine could be. Today, the style is swinging away from heavy-handed oak towards a more restrained wine. Cooler-climate sites are yielding grapes with higher acidity and more subtle flavors – not only is the buttery oak toned down, but so is the ultra-ripe peach and pineapple fruit. Regionally, the most impressive new-wave Aussie Chardonnays are coming from the Adelaide Hills, Margaret River, Southern Victoria and Tasmania. Those who like blockbusters will still find them – Hunter Valley Chardonnay is usually pretty full-on.

Austria

The most exciting Austrian wines are made from its native varieties, but Chardonnay is there too. The best wine hails from Styria (where it's also called Morillon) and Wachau. Surprisingly rich and ripe, they usually come with a hefty dose of sawdusty oak.

Canada

Canadian Chardonnay is a rare sight away from its home turf, but try the wines from British Columbia and Ontario if you get the opportunity – they can be classy, fresh and fruity.

Chile

Chilean Chardonnay is usually a great buy – at the lower end of the price spectrum you can count on it for bright, simple wine, with delicious tropical fruit flavors and crisp acidity to balance. A big success, then, although the more expensive Chilean efforts sometimes fail to thrill. Watch for top wines from the cool Casablanca Valley.

Eastern Europe

Bulgaria and Hungary make sound identikit Chardonnays, usually clean, soft and mildly oaky. Heartwarmingly cheap if you like this style.

France

Burgundy is Chardonnay's spiritual home and, despite the best efforts of an international posse of winemakers, it still sets the standard by which the others are measured. Is it what it's

...white burgundy is a heavenly experience. The vineyards are divided into minuscule plots and the best wines reflect their subtle differences in microclimate and soil...

cracked up to be? At its best, white burgundy (don't look for 'Chardonnay' on the label – you won't find it) is a heavenly experience. The vineyards are divided into minuscule plots and the best wines reflect their subtle differences in microclimate and soil. The Chablis and Côte d'Or regions produce benchmark Chardonnays of wonderful finesse, where honey, nuts and spices are melded seamlessly with fresh, vivacious fruit flavors. Then again, plenty of mediocre, dull wines are also made in Burgundy, especially in the Mâconnais, so tread carefully. Find a reputable merchant (or better still, a grower) that you like and stick to your guns. Many of the greatest wines come from Puligny-Montrachet, Meursault and Chassagne-Montrachet. In Champagne, Chardonnay is one of the three grapes used (see page 72), and in the south of France, well-priced *vin de pays* Chardonnay is made in the sunny, ripe manner of the New World.

Italy

Italian Chardonnay runs the gamut from the crisp, light (and, frankly, sometimes boring) wines of Friuli in the northeast, to a fruity, modern style favored in Piedmont to the west. Further south, some Tuscan producers are turning out richly oaked premium wines, many of which are meant to be taken terribly seriously. Sicily's new-wave wines are better value.

New Zealand

Its most famous white wines are made from Sauvignon, but don't overlook New Zealand's well-balanced, fruit-driven Chardonnays. The Marlborough,

Nelson and Canterbury areas (South Island) each make excellent examples, stamped with the same pure, clean fruit flavor that all the top Kiwi whites appear to have. This time it's lemons and oranges all the way, rather than the relentless gooseberry of Sauvignon. Chardonnays from the

Don't overlook New Zealand's well-balanced, fruit-driven Chardonnays...This time it's lemons and oranges all the way, rather than the relentless gooseberry of Sauvignon

warmer North Island tend to be richer and more tropical, especially those from Gisborne. Hawke's Bay is another region that's enjoying success with this grape.

Portugal
Not a country that is crazy for Chardonnay (a refreshing change), Portugal's street-wise winemakers nonetheless make a little (rich, ripe, fairly oaky) to satisfy export markets.

South Africa
Some of the most refined wines to emerge from the Cape of late are Chardonnays. The sunny fruit flavors are delicious, and oak is used with increasing skill. The warm Paarl region

produces rich wines; the cooler, coastal Walker Bay area makes a more restrained, Burgundian version, while wines from Robertson are arguably the best of the lot, with real elegance and a mineral streak – the result of stony, lime-rich sites and low yields.

Spain
Heavily oaked white Riojas are wonderfully unfashionable, so try the well-balanced, subtle Chardonnays from other areas for something more modern. Navarra and Somontano are the most promising (northern) regions.

USA
Americans just lovvve Chardonnay. Good thing they make such great wine from it then, especially in California, where top labels rank alongside the very best from France and Australia. Bear in mind we're talking big, ripe, peachy flavors, and a good dollop of rich oak – the fruit is so fleshy and generous, it can stand up to the oak in a powerful, well-balanced union. Expect a scary price tag. Californians have also realised biggest isn't always best, and more elegant styles are emanating from cooler sub-regions. At the cheaper end, California doesn't compete so well. Try premium wines from Oregon, Washington State, and, if you can find them, Long Island.

Sauvignon Blanc

Great white hope or a bit of a joke?

Er, both, actually. For many, Sauvignon Blanc conjures up several contrasting images. It's the grape variety behind some of the most haughtily elegant, refined whites in the world, from France's Loire Valley. Further south, it plays a major role in Bordeaux's greatest dry and sweet white wines, and all over the southwest of France it contributes to some of the most popular inexpensive dry whites. Sometimes these are oaked to provide a richer, fuller wine.

CELLAR, GLASS & PLATE

Storing: Simple, light Sauvignons need drinking up quickly, before they lose their youthful fresh appeal. But richer, riper styles last well. Older New Zealand Sauvignon can be a pleasant surprise and fine, oaked Sauvignon-Sémillon blends from Bordeaux really benefit from a few years in bottle.

Serving: Mouth-tingling Sauvignon makes a brilliant *apéritif*... serve chilled.

Food matching: Great with grilled white fish, tomato dishes, mild cheeses (especially goat's), sweet-tasting shellfish such as scallops, and even asparagus.

New World wine fans go crazy for a glass of aromatic, gooseberry-packed Kiwi Sauvignon, especially if the label happens to have the magic words 'Cloudy Bay' on it. In fact, New Zealand Sauvignon is a giveaway at blind tastings – a true modern classic, you can tell it a mile off. So, a fine and versatile grape then. It's just the cat's piss that causes problems.

Sorry? Spray that again?

Cat's piss. Tom-cat spray to be precise. And sweaty armpits. And tomato leaves. And asparagus. Not really what you expect, or indeed want, to waft up from a glass of crisp white wine. And yet, for every two bottles of clean, pure, crisp and lemony Sauvignon, there's a savory, catty one. Sauvignon Blanc can certainly be a challenge. For everyone who loves a truly feline example, there are plenty who would rather put something that pungent out for the night.

Well, we think sharp, savory Sauvignon is great. It just takes some getting used to. The worst Sauvignons, in our view, are weak and dilute ones (due to high yields) or those made with unripe fruit, which taste, as one New Zealand

winemaker put it, like a 'lean, green grass-cutting machine'. No, this grape needs ripeness and intensity to express itself – to scratch at the door, yowl at the moon, piddle in the corner.

What about blends?

Sauvignon makes excellent single varietal wines, but in France it is often used in partnership with the fatter Sémillon. This makes a lot of sense. The Sauvignon Blanc fruit provides the racy acidity and zesty aroma, while the Sémillon fills out this lean, somewhat spiky character with a richer, fuller texture. This ideal pairing crops up in the great white wines of Bordeaux (both dry and sweet) and in everyday guzzling whites from the southwest of France (such as cheap Entre-Deux-Mers or Bergerac). A dab of scented Muscadelle is sometimes added too.

In the Loire Valley and the New World, Sauvignon is more often encountered on its own, although a few wineries in the former blend it with the other local hero, Chenin Blanc, and a few in the latter blend it with Chardonnay. Neither marriage is particularly successful. Sémillon is the undisputed ideal partner here.

From gooseberries to cat's pee. Spray that again...

Australia

Not the Aussies' ace card. It's a little too warm in many regions to make properly crisp Sauvignon Blanc, but there are some exceptions emerging from cooler spots such as Tasmania and the Adelaide Hills. Here, the grape's acidity remains snappy and fresh. Still, expect a fruity, fairly ripe style. It's sometimes blended with Sémillon to make an ultra-fruity wine (which works nicely) or with Chardonnay (which doesn't really, in our book).

Austria

Ever tried Austrian Sauvignon? If not, you're missing out. It's mainly made in the region of Styria, to the south of the country. Bracing acidity, a certain steeliness, even a mineral quality, plus pure lemony fruit means it is almost as refreshing as a trip down a ski slope.

California

Heavy, rich Fumé Blanc (oaked, off-dry, frequently flabby Sauvignon Blanc, its name redolent of its smokey-oaky note) is one of California's signature wine styles, although it's now way out of fashion and in our view misses the whole point of the grape, which is its tight-knit, crisp quality. Today fresher, zingier and generally finer Sauvignons are starting to emerge from prime, cool-climate spots on the West Coast, thankfully.

Chile

The Chileans make impressive, beautifully balanced, gooseberry-scented Sauvignon in cooler spots such as the Casablanca Valley, plus some more pungent wines in other areas. Acidity tends to be high, so

Grab one produced in the Marlborough region if you need a wake-up call for the nose and palate...as thrilling a jolt to the senses as a bungee jump off Mount Cook.

expect a zippy, succulent style. Tread carefully, though, as in the past they have ripped us off with a cheaper and poorer grape variety called Sauvignonasse, which tastes like Sauvignon when young, but dies on its 'ass' in no time and loses all its fruit flavor in the bottle. Stick to well-known, reputable producers.

Eastern Europe

Some aromatic, rather savory, bone-dry Sauvignons from Hungary are worthwhile, especially as they are so well-priced. They give New Zealand's cheaper offerings a run for their money. Bulgaria makes some Sauvignon, but its quality varies alarmingly. Occasionally a decent Romanian Sauvignon pops up, but not often.

France

Loire Valley Now you're talking. Great Sancerre or Pouilly-Fumé from the Loire is so pure, clean and serene it could enroll as a nun. Less well-known, but potentially just as good, are Sauvignons from the neighboring regions of Quincy, Reuilly and Menetou-Salon. Think crisp, grassy, lemony notes, bone dry with a faint whiff of gun-smoke. Clear water running over grey pebbles, a glint of cool sun through the ripples.... Top wines often come from limestone-heavy vineyards. These bottles make for some of the most mouthwatering, refreshing and elegant *apéritifs* ever.

Bordeaux and southwest France

Here Sauvignon's usually blended with Sémillon and perhaps a little Muscadelle to create aromatic dry whites with a grassy quality and rounded citrus character. Some are simple, lively whites, but the top wines are richer and carefully oaked. Sauvignon here also plays an important part in majestic, honeyed dessert wines (see page 90).

Other good-value French Sauvignons include sprightly, racy Sauvignon de Touraine from the eastern Loire, varietal Sauvignon Blanc from

Bergerac in the southwest, or *vins de pays* with Sauvignon on the label. Of the latter, Vin de Pays du Jardin de la France (from the Loire area) is your best bet.

Italy

Northern Italian Sauvignons, particularly from the scenic, often high altitude regions of Friuli-Venezia-Giulia and Alto-Adige, conjure up the freshness and purity of cool mountain air. Nice – but pretty rare and often pricey.

New Zealand

New Zealand's super-star Sauvignons are really pungent, with bags of ripe gooseberry and hints of herbs, tomato leaf, green capsicum and the odd 'meow' from our furry friend. Grab one produced in the Marlborough region of the South Island if you need a wake-up call for the nose and palate. Expect a rush of green fruit and mouthwatering acidity on the finish – as thrilling a jolt to the senses as a bungee jump off the top of Mount Cook!

Brilliant as they are, these extrovert, outspoken wines can get a little tiresome after a while. Fortunately, some more subtle examples are now coming on to the market. Standards are currently high, and the benchmark wine from Sauvignon pioneer Cloudy Bay now faces a serious challenge from other, less pricey, labels.

South Africa

Sauvignon's not the first grape variety that springs to mind when you think of South Africa, but the Cape crusaders have been working hard on the grape and, mainly due to better site selection, now turn out some world-beating bottles. There are carefully balanced wines, with the mineral notes and fresh acidity of the Old World, plus a more New World-like hint of succulent passionfruit. The best come from the regions of Constantia right by Cape Town, Elgin, and the limestone-rich soils of Robertson, further inland. You'll be impressed.

Spain

Not a lot of this grape variety is grown in Spain. But track down the zappy, crisp, herbaceous whites of the Rueda region in the center of the country to see how recent use of Sauvignon Blanc – either alone or in a blend with local grape Verdejo – has improved the Spanish style and brought the wines into the modern age of winemaking.

Riesling

Isn't that the Liebfraumilch grape?
No. Lovely Lieb is almost always made from cheaper, lesser white grapes. And a totally different variety, Welschriesling, is responsible for the dubious delights of central European cheapie Laski Rizling.

Real Riesling (sometimes called Rhine Riesling) is behind some of the world's finest white wines. In fact, many connoisseurs argue that it is the best white grape of all. In cooler climates, where the Riesling vine weathers the winter temperatures well, this is certainly the case. But it's pointless to choose between Riesling and, say, Chardonnay as champion: they each have an important role to play and it's best to sample both.

So, if you've rejected Riesling in the past, be broad-minded! Try some of Germany's top wines, or a fuller-bodied classic from Alsace. You'll discover real Riesling runs the gamut between piercingly fresh and dry and wonderfully honeyed and sweet. Riesling is hypersensitive to its *terroir* (the site, soil, sun, rain etc of the location where it is grown), which is brought out particularly clearly in the character of the finished wine. So it's satisfying to taste through a range and spot the differences between wines of different origin. When you get to the New World, you can expect racy, lime-drenched wines – in fact, about the liveliest, most refreshing New World whites you can buy.

Cheap and nasty?
The cheapest, most dilute Rieslings are disappointing, but quality Riesling is a revelation. First of all, the elegant, floral aroma can be exquisite. The high acidity and steely austerity of very young, dry Riesling can send a shiver down your spine, but under the sharpness lies a remarkably delicate, pretty lacework of flavors: orchard and citrus fruits, especially apples, oranges and lemons. Then, with age, the crispness softens, the freshly chopped fruit turns more mellow and honeyed, and a distinct aroma of petrol, or lanolin, or toast, appears. The amazing longevity of fine Riesling is another key asset.

OK, OK, so it's wonder-fuel...
It's not only the mistaken association with cheaper, blander wines that puts us off, it's also that Riesling often comes in unfashionable tall, green bottles with horribly complex labels. Riesling is cloaked in arcane language (maybe so the wine buffs can save the best for themselves) but we've answered a lot of Riesling riddles here.

CELLAR, GLASS & PLATE

Storing: European Riesling is incredibly long-lived, so squirrel away a few bottles for a decade or more.

Serving: With its mouthwatering acidity, fresh fruit flavors and low alcohol, dry or off-dry Riesling is a great *apéritif* – serve it chilled.

Matching with food: Great with subtly spicy, light Thai and Asian-fusion dishes which rely on fresh, aromatic ingredients. Off-dry styles work with Chinese food. Crisp, dry wines cut through fat well, so try baked cheese dishes or roast pork. Sweet Riesling is brilliant with fruit puddings!

Put petrol in your motor

Australia

Aussie Riesling, as you would imagine, tastes quite different to any other. This is Riesling with a Bondi Beach suntan. From the most important Riesling regions of South Australia – the Clare and Eden valleys – young wines have a juicy lime aroma and ripe, fruit-driven flavor. With age they take on a rich lanolin and toasty, honeyed character – Aussie Rieslings rarely smell of gasoline, like their European counterparts. Crisper, pure-tasting, more mineral-tangy Rieslings are made in Tasmania's cool-climate vineyards, and some excellent, ripe and fruity examples are produced in Western Australia. Occasionally Riesling is blended with other white grapes, such as Gewürztraminer, but really it's much better on its own.

Austria

Steely dry Riesling (aka Weisser Riesling or Rheinriesling) is one of Austria's most successful styles. The most important region for the variety is the Wachau, in Lower Austria, where the Riesling is bone dry, clean and fragrant, with a mineral, almost steely quality. It ages well for years. In the great dessert wine region of Neusiedlersee in Burgenland, Riesling is one of several grapes used to make nobly rotten sweet wines to an exceptionally high standard.

Canada

They may be underrated and not readily available on the export market, but Canada's Rieslings are well worth trying. Both dry and sweet ('Eiswein') styles are made, and the best wines are produced in the state of Ontario.

France

Alsace, to be precise – Riesling is rarely grown elsewhere in France. For some, Alsace Riesling is even better

We promise, once you sample a fine Riesling from the Mosel on a hot summer's day, you will never, ever go back to bland German cheapies...

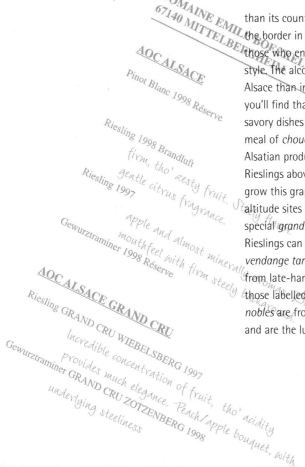

GERALD TAYLOR
13 Aircraft Esplanade
HANTS GU 14 6TG Farnborough

DOMAINE EMIL BOE
67140 MITTELBERGHEIM

AOC ALSACE

Pinot Blanc 1998 Réserve

Riesling 1998 Brandluft
firm, tho' zesty fruit. Steely fr...

Riesling 1997
gentle citrus fragrance.

Gewurztraminer 1998 Réserve
apple and almost mineral(?) mouthfeel with firm steely ba..kayo Delic...

AOC ALSACE GRAND CRU

Riesling GRAND CRU WIEBELSBERG 1997
Incredible concentration of fruit, tho' acidity provides much elegance. Peach/apple bouquet, with

Gewurztraminer GRAND CRU ZOTZENBERG 1998
underlying steeliness

than its counterpart made just over the border in Germany. It will suit those who enjoy a fragrant but richer style. The alcohol level is higher in Alsace than in German Rieslings and you'll find that it matches heartier savory dishes – try it with a full-on meal of *choucroute*. Many top Alsatian producers prize their top Rieslings above any other wines, and grow this grape in their best, higher-altitude sites (often vineyards given special *grand cru* status). While the Rieslings can be dry or off-dry, *vendange tardive* are sweeter, made from late-harvested grapes, while those labelled *sélection des grains nobles* are from nobly rotten berries and are the luscious sweet styles.

Germany

Although Germany continues to fail at the very bottom of the price spectrum for white wines, its finest bottles are as thrilling (and, ironically, as fairly priced) as ever. And they are nearly all made from Riesling. Whether it's an airily light, fruity, apple-blossom scented Mosel Riesling, or a pure, zesty Nahe example; a full-flavored, modern one from the Pfalz or an intense, steely version from the Rheingau, German Riesling from its various regions deserves far, far more respect from the general public. Connoisseurs love it, but yer average wine drinker still looks askance when presented with a bottle of German Riesling, which is a strange state of affairs. We promise, once you sample a fine Riesling from the Mosel on a hot summer's day, you will never go back to bland German cheapies made from the inferior Müller-Thurgau grape.

Many German wines are slightly sweetened with unfermented grape juice; others are bone dry. How can you tell which is which? Tough call. The words Trocken (dry) and Halbtrocken (medium dry) on a label help a little. And the best-quality wines (labelled QmP) are divided into six categories according to the ripeness of the grapes at harvest. These categories guide you towards the style of wine – kind of: Kabinett tends to be dry, Spätlese is off-dry (or extra-ripe; some Spätleses are sweeter than others), Auslese roughly corresponds to our idea of medium, Beerenauslese is distinctly sweet, Trockenbeerenauslese is extremely sweet, and Eiswein is ludicrously sweet.

Italy

A few light, racy, zesty, dry Rieslings are made in Italy, mainly at the top of the country in the cooler northeastern regions of Friuli, Trentino and Alto Adige. It's refreshing stuff but it tends to lack complexity.

Aussie Riesling, as you would imagine, tastes quite different to any other. This is Riesling with a Bondi Beach suntan...

New Zealand

Riesling has only been well-established in New Zealand since the 1980s, but those from the cool, sunny Marlborough region in the South Island are already a joy, with their dry style, mineral extract, fresh, light fruitiness and crisp finish. Impressive late-harvest sweet wines are also made in New Zealand.

South Africa

Not the Cape's ace card, but several good-quality, citrus-fresh Rieslings, both dry and sweet, are produced, sometimes with the name Weisser Riesling on the label.

South America

Argentina and Chile both produce a few snappy, dry Rieslings, usually with attractive citrus fruit flavors, but it could be taken more seriously in both countries. Who will make the first premium South American Riesling?

USA

Riesling is grown in the cool areas around the Finger Lakes, in northern NY, where it is one of the few grapes to weather the cold winters. You may have to go there to try it, as little moves out of the state. Oregon and Washington Rieslings have made more impact on international drinkers. Oregon, which has a damp, cool climate, comes up with elegant, complex dry wines in good vintages (and weak, flabby ones in poor years). Washington's top Rieslings, like all the state's best white wines, have a pure, clean, fruity character.

Sémillon

Sémillon who?

Sémillon is a modest grape, one that seems almost embarrassed to be given full single varietal status. It's versatile, but instead of courting publicity it gets on with the job quietly. If it were an actor it would be Alec Guinness.

What, like an ageing Jedi knight?

No. More like the d'Ascoyne family he played in *Kind Hearts and Coronets*. Sémillon can be bone dry and unoaked, ripe and oak aged, rich and sweet. It plays different roles, but has hidden depths. When young, the wines can seem hard and stony, but it mellows with time — and can cope with oak.

The force is with it?

It's pretty impressive. That's all down to another similarity with actors. A thin skin. Botrytis rot (a mold which can attack the grape, producing affected bunches which give some of the world's greatest sweet wines) doesn't need a second invitation to creep up into the vineyards of Sauternes in the morning mist and eat away at Sémillon's covering. Even when it's made dry, Sémillon's texture is refreshingly different, with a viscosity that isn't necessarily sweet, but coats the mouth. It's creamy but not a fat butterball. Honeyed and soft, but with a vegetal note. The Bordelais stop it getting too fat by blending it with racy Sauvignon Blanc.

So why haven't we heard of it?

The French believe the region is always more important than the name of the grape. Other countries aren't so shy.

Aha, those Aussies again?

Spot on. We sometimes wonder if, at the start of the Aussie white wine boom, Riverlands producers needed something to make Chardonnay go further and a container-load of Sémillon turned up at the right time. Today, Sém-Chard is an unremarkable easy-quaffing, mass-market wine that gives you no great desire to try the grape on its own: a shame.

So yet another 'forgotten classic'?

Oz's top Sémillon-Sauvignons from Margaret River restore the faith. And if you want to see what Sémillon can do under its own steam choose from two Aussie camps: the unoaked Hunter Valley wines and oak-aged wines from Clare and Barossa. There are also great late-harvest examples. Young Hunter Sémillon is lean and as grassy as a newly-mown football field. Leave it five, 10 or 20 years and something bizarre happens. It turns toasty, almost as if it's been languishing in an oak barrel. Schizo – in a nice way.

CELLAR, GLASS & PLATE

Storing: Stash Australian Hunter Valley Sémillon away for years (or buy museum releases that have been stashed away for you). Barossan examples also age superbly well, gaining in honey and nuttiness as they mature.

Serving: Lightly chilled is best for any Sémillon.

Matching with food: As ever, it depends on the style, but young Hunter Valley and moderately oaked Barossa Valley wines work well with fish and seafood dishes.

Schizo – in a nice way

Australia

Everyone's got to know Chardonnay but they haven't bothered with Sémillon and that's a shame because the regional styles show so well. In the Hunter Valley, early-picking, no oak and no malolactic fermentation (which softens wine and adds complexity), give a young, almost neutral dry wine; leave it a decade in bottle and out pours liquid buttered wholemeal toast smothered with lime marmalade. It's one of the great wines of the world! Then, in the Barossa Valley, there's a bigger, barrel-aged, barrel-fermented style; the top wines have a steely limey acidity which keeps them fresh. Sémillons from Clare follow in this toasty vein, while those from cool-climate Lenswood are leaner (and cleaner). In Western Australia, Margaret River is home to the country's greatest red 'Bordeaux blends', so no surprise that producers also blend Sémillon with Sauvignon; powerful, limey with herbal-fennel aromas.

France

Bordeaux Great dry Bordeaux white can be stunningly good – round in the mouth with lemon acidity, apples and a smooth texture that becomes nutty and honeyed as it matures. Look for Graves or Pessac-Léognan on the label, but expect to empty your piggy bank to afford the best.

Sauternes/Barsac Sauternes and Barsac are among the world's greatest and most long-lived sweet wines (see page 90). Botrytis-affected Sémillon gives a waxy richness, while Sauvignon chips in with cheeky, fresh acidity.

Rest of the World

In America, look to Washington State where dry Sémillon has proved to be a perfect partner for seafood and funky 'fusion' cooking. At one time South Africa grew nothing else, but it didn't make good brandy, so out it came. Now there's one (magnificent) example – from Boekenhoutskloof. Sémillon's widely grown in Chile, where it makes astonishingly dreary dry wine.

Chenin Blanc

Ah yes, the South African grape...

Well yes, Chenin *is* the most widely planted white variety in SA, but the grape's home is the Loire Valley, France, specifically in the middle section of the river. If Sauvignon holds sway near the source, and Melon de Bourgogne at the mouth, then the tranquil central part is Chenin's patch. Given the French reluctance for naming varieties on the label, Chenin hides its light under a bushel – or a woolly blanket.

You're at it again...

The thing is, Chenin has great acidity and can have a needle-sharp lime attack, with green apple fruit upper-most, but behind that there's a strange wet wool, lanolin-like aroma, like your sweater after you've been caught in the rain. It's a smell of damp dogs, the straw and soggy sheep... maybe it's wet sheepdog! Then there can be some lactic, baby-sick notes as well.

Sounds lovely

Stay with us, stay with us. Chenin has naturally high acidity, which means it needs to get ripe, but if it's in too hot a climate it ends up being like a doughnut – there's nothing in the middle of the mouth. Badly-made

CELLAR, GLASS & PLATE

Storing: Dry can need seven years; sweet...well, anything from 15 to over 50 years.

Serving: Lightly chilled.

Matching with food: Drink dry Loire Chenin with light fish, fish and chips, seafood, salads, even Thai food. The best South African Chenins are easy-drinking wines that slip down a treat with almost anything. Sweet styles go very well with fruit-laden desserts.

Chenin is easy to spot, but the best? Well, that lanolin gives way to waxiness, then to honey, all wrapped round exotic fruits and always with that nervy, preserving, acidity which allows Chenin to be among the white wine world's most long-lived wines. Chenin is also susceptible to botrytis, which allows the grape to make some of the world's greatest, most venerable and overlooked sweet wines. Nowhere are these qualities better seen than in the Loire Valley.

So it's versatile?

Chenin can be made piercingly dry, medium sweet, or full-on, botrytis-affected sweet. So it's versatile, and it's also like Riesling insofar as few people have realised what a superb, idiosyncratically wonderful grape it can be. It's great news for the adventurous drinker, though Chenin has one other tricky characteristic. You have to tread carefully to be sure which level of sweetness you are buying. That's where we come in to help. Go on, give Chenin a try. You'll probably never look at Chardonnay again!

Any style, any place, anywhere

Australia

Chenin's never evolved into anything more than an everyday blender, picked early to give an acid bite to anonymous dry white blends.

California

Chenin's ignored here as well, a Central Valley workhorse destined for cheap dry blends, fortifieds and brandy.

France

Anjou The central part of the Loire and the home of basic Chenin-based, rather average, dry Anjou Blanc.

Bonnezeaux One of the Loire's finest sweet wine areas, where wines are usually affected by botrytis (see p90).

Coteaux du Layon Here Chenin can be medium-dry (*demi-sec*), sweet (*moelleux*) or very sweet (*liquoreux*) (see p90–91). The best show Chenin to be powerful, ageless and elegant but be careful, there's a lot of dross.

Quarts de Chaume Like Bonnezeaux, an enclave within Coteaux du Layon. Minuscule production of botrytised Chenin.

Savennières One of the few Loire areas making intense, dry Chenin Blanc. Stash it away a good few years.

Vouvray Chenin's home. Vouvray can be sweet, medium-dry, dry or sparkling. It always has searingly high acidity, and often needs decades to open, but be patient and one of the world's greatest wines may emerge. (It can also be cheap and nasty).

New Zealand

Beginning to get to grips with this grape. Watch this space.

South Africa

Chenin was planted here for brandy, so most is in the wrong place for winemaking. It is usually boring stuff and many winemakers have dug it up, but some are persevering. With old vines and hands-on winemaking, maybe even barrel fermenting, it's worth the attention. It's fatter and more tropical than most – a dry wine.

Viognier

Viognier, the 'New Chardonnay...'?

Is utterly, fantastically, fashionable daahhling. As hip as Gucci, as chic as Agnès B. Why? That's a bit like asking why hemlines rise and fall, though we reckon a lot of it is down to the fact that Viognier's original stomping ground, the Northern Rhône, has itself become one of the most fashionable wine regions in the world. When the Rhône star was in the ascendent, everything associated with it rose in people's estimation, even a half-forgotten, obscure variety like Viognier. Equally, it has such an incredible aroma that after one sniff, winemakers around the world fell under its spell. Whatever the case, Viognier has been plucked from the chorus line like Alice Faye in a 1920s musical.

An exhibitionist then?

In terms of aroma, this certainly isn't a variety that's slow about coming forward. It doesn't so much seduce you as launch a full-out perfumed assault on the senses. There's bouquets of aromatic flowers such as freesia, honeysuckle and May blossom, rich overipe peach and apricots dripping with juice, and a touch of vanilla pod. It's like walking past a branch of the Body Shop on a hot summer's day.

So why isn't there more of it?

This is where it goes all bashful and awkward. Viognier flowers unevenly, can be shy and doesn't ripen evenly. It also needs to hang on to the vine for a long time to get fully ripe and develop those famous heady aromas. You don't want it to over-crop either. If you want to capture that incredible scent, you have to keep yields low and concentrate it within a few bunches. High yields of over-ripe Viognier give a pretty boring fat white wine.

Sounds tricky

It's a bit of a paradox. Here you have an aromatic grape that only develops its full varietal character when it's bursting with sugar (although the wines are dry as the sugar turns to alcohol). Winemakers have to aim for a kind of restrained hedonism which lets the wonderful exotic scents unfold without the wine flopping over into flabbiness and high levels of alcohol.

Is wood no good?

Opinion is divided, but most winemakers agree that putting Viognier in new oak tends to over-complicate matters. Viognier is to white wine what Pinot Noir is to red: it's fickle in the vineyard, only performs in certain sites and is expensive. It takes an obsessive winemaker to try and perfect it.

CELLAR, GLASS & PLATE

Storing: If you like a big, heavy wine put Viognier away, otherwise drink it quickly. Most prefer it with some youthful crispness.

Serving: Lightly chilled is best.

Matching with food: Drink chilled Viognier on its own, or match it with chicken in creamy sauces, or mild fruity curries. It's too peachy and rich for fish dishes.

Richer than Gates, more perfumed than Gabor

Australia

Plantings remain small and so far only those wines from the Eden Valley are showing any degree of complexity.

France

Viognier's home is in the Northern Rhône, where the tiny enclave of Condrieu and the even smaller Château-Grillet saved the grape from extinction. The best Viogniers in the world still hail from Condrieu vineyards. Drink the wines when young and swoon over the aroma. Viognier is sometimes blended in with Syrah in the local red wines, such as Côte-Rôtie, to give a perfumed lift.

Château-Grillet may be small, but scarcity doesn't always equal quality. The new pioneers of the Languedoc have leapt on the grape with great glee and huge plantings have taken place in recent years. The wines haven't yet reached the heady depths of the Northern Rhône, but they do offer a lightly perfumed (and low-priced) introduction to the style.

USA

California's 'Rhône Rangers' are beginning to master Viognier, and Mendocino, Sonoma and Santa Barbara have emerged as the main centers. Some are still making it big and over-oaked, but the best producers have managed to hit that tricky balance between needing high levels of ripeness without making the wines too fat and flabby. Unfortunately, many growers are starting to feel that Rousanne is the white Rhône grape to concentrate on.

More white grapes

A few years ago, some wag in the wine trade came up with the acronym ABC – 'Anything But Chardonnay' . Anyone who has ever felt as though they were drowning under a tidal wave of same-ish oaky New World Chardonnay will know exactly why it is important to explore other styles of white wine thoroughly. Wine drinking should always be about diversity, so try to ring the changes as much as possible and discover some new flavors – if you don't, then you can't complain if Chardonnay vines eventually stretch their tendrils right across the world, like an army of ants.

Sauvignon Blanc and Riesling are grapes you probably already know. But there are plenty of other, lesser-known white varieties which provide a thrill or two. And, of course, some very mediocre ones that are to blame for all the dross out there. Here is a selection of the ones you are most likely to encounter, for better or for worse...

The support team

Albariño
Iberian star. Produces Spain's best dry whites – ripe, aromatic, peach-and-lime flavored wines from the Rías Baixas, at the western tip of the country. Also crops up as Alvarinho in Northern Portugal's Vinho Verde country, making some of the more acceptable wines of the region. Albariño is a thick-skinned grape which rots less easily than some – good news for the vine growers in these damp Atlantic coast regions of Iberia.

Aligoté
The 'also-ran' white grape of Burgundy, which makes light, tart, simple dry wines – pleasant, easy-drinking stuff, but watch out for leanness and high acidity. Or try a local tradition and mix it with sweet crème de cassis to make kir. Some riper, creamier, more serious Aligotés are made in warmer years.

Colombard
Colombard's roots are in southwest France, where it was originally used

to make brandy. Now it's a workhorse grape for inexpensive, easy-drinking dry whites, sometimes blended with Ugni Blanc (together they make Vin de Pays des Côtes de Gascogne). In South Africa and California, it's behind plain, everyday quaffing wines, both dry and off-dry. Sometimes used as a cheap blending partner for Chardonnay.

Gewürztraminer

Imagine soaking a box of Turkish Delight in a vat of rosewater, adding litchi and peach essence, a sprinkling of powdered ginger and fermenting the result. 'Gewürz' is a heady mix of exotic perfume and rich tropical fruits – you either love it or loathe it. Fans swear by ripe, almost oily-rich Alsace Gewürz, which ranges from dry to deeply luscious and sweet. If you want a lighter, crisper style, try one from Germany, Northern Italy, Chile, New Zealand or even Hungary. Oh, and try it with spicy fish dishes, especially Thai-style.

Grüner Veltliner

It's never likely to become a big star, but Austria's Grüner Veltliner, with its distinctive white pepper and grapefruit zest character, can be delicious, and a refreshing change from endless bottles of Chardonnay

and Sauvignon Blanc. Most GVs are made in a crisp, dry and simple style, so drink 'em up while they are youthful and bright. The more serious, weighty wines from top Austrian growers will last a few years.

Malvasia

Think Frascati is boring? It would be even worse if it wasn't for Malvasia perking up the blend. Malvasia adds fragrance and a fruity tang to a dull grape like Trebbiano in well-known Italian whites. It also pops up in Northern Spain, Portugal and California. And if you drink a tasty local dry white while on holiday in the Canary Islands, chances are it's made from this variety.

Marsanne

Blended with Roussanne to make the white wines of the Northern Rhône – Saint-Joseph, Hermitage, Crozes-Hermitage, Saint-Péray. Don't expect fresh fruit salad flavors. Instead, look out for richly textured, deeply colored dry whites with a slight nuttiness, perhaps a hint of aniseed and sometimes a whiff of peach kernel. Marsanne is also grown in the south of France and it is occasionally produced in a richly oaked style in Australia and a silky one in California.

Melon de Bourgogne

If it wasn't for this grape, there would be no Muscadet. Shame. To be fair, the neutral, tart, vaguely appley Melon de Bourgogne has been coaxed into making some half-decent wines. Anyone who has tried a superior Muscadet, with creamy, yeasty depths, will have a good word for it. Rarely, if ever, seen outside France's Loire Valley.

Müller-Thurgau

Müller-Thurgau makes Melon de Bourgogne look positively racy. This is the grape (the culprit) behind most

If you haven't tried the Tokay-Pinot Gris of Alsace, you're missing out on a richly textured, smokey, spicy white that's brilliant with heart-busting, fatty French cuisine...

cheap, bland, off-dry German whites (no, it's not Riesling's fault), and yet more boring wines from Austria, Italy, central and eastern Europe, England, and even New Zealand. Oddly popular a generation ago, growers and winemakers have now, thankfully, seen sense and it is considered pretty outmoded.

Muscat

The Muscats (a large family including Muscat of Alexandria, Muscat-à-Petits Grains, Muscat Ottonel) are a versatile lot. As well as producing a wide range of dessert wines and sparklers (see pages 90 and 70), they make mouthwatering, fresh, dry Muscat, with its characteristic perfume of crunchy green grapes, in southern France, Alsace, Northern Italy and Austria.

Pinot Blanc

Big in Alsace, where its wines are soft, fruity and food friendly. Germans and Austrians call it Weissburgunder and make anything from simple, acidic, dry whites to richer, oaked, also dry wines from it. In Italy, as Pinot Bianco, it is popular for whites and sparklers. It's also found in California.

Pinot Gris

Best known as the mediocre Italian Pinot Grigio to many, although if you haven't tried the Tokay-Pinot Gris of Alsace (strange name; same grape) you're missing out on a richly textured, smokey, spicy, dry white that's brilliant with pâté, confit, and other heart-busting, fatty French cuisine. Try German and Austrian takes on the same grape (aka Grauburgunder and Ruländer), and definitely give the impressive New World versions made in Oregon a whirl.

Roussanne

Aromatic grape, with a hint of gingery warmth and snappy acidity, that usually puts in its appearance

...we've included Scheurebe because we like it...it tastes emphatically of grapefruit and is known in Austria as Samling 88, so now you know.

married to Marsanne: the two of them blend together to make Northern Rhône dry whites (they also go into some of the reds to round them out). Roussanne appears in the blend for white Châteauneuf-du-Pape, pops up in the South of France and, now and again, in Australia and California.

Scheurebe

Not well-known, but we've included it because we like this German grape.. At its best it has a tangy, racy, zesty quality, tastes emphatically of grapefruit – clean, crisp and fresh. It makes luscious sweet wines too. It's known in Austria as Samling 88, so now you know.

Trebbiano

Aka Ugni Blanc in France. It's hard to work up much enthusiasm for this tedious high-yielding grape, which produces so much crisp, light, but ultimately forgettable, European dry wine. In France it makes brandy as well as cheap white in the southwest, and in Italy it bulks out the blends for Orvieto, Frascati, Soave and others. Not much grown in the New World – producers there look for more flavor!

Viura

A characterless, faintly floral variety sometimes called Macabeo – both names are used in Spain, where you are most likely to come across this grape. Important in Rioja for light, less traditional white wines than usual, and in Penedès as one of a trio of grapes used for cava. Also found across the border in deepest southwest France, where it plays a part in blends.

White wine styles

NAME	REGION	COUNTRY	GRAPE	TASTE	PRICE	ANYTHING ELSE?
Cape Country White	The Cape, stoopid	South Africa	Mainly Chenin Blanc and Colombard	Can be neutral and bland, even off-dry and flabby, but the best are fruity and bright with succulent lemon and lime flavor. Good party white	$	Should please a crowd – of non-wine buffs
Chablis	Burgundy	France	Chardonnay	Elegant, restrained style of Chardonnay, green-gold in color, often with steely, mineral note. Oak is used sparingly and the fruit flavor leans towards apple	$$–$$$	Modern Chablis is more fruity and rounded than in the past
Condrieu	Northern Rhône	France	Viognier	Essence of ripe apricots, deeply aromatic, weighty and rich with heady notes of honeysuckle and peach skin. Late summer in a glass	$$$	Made in tiny quantities and not easy to find – a cult wine for rich collectors
Côtes de Gascogne	Southwest	France	Ugni Blanc and Colombard	Crisp, unoaked and grassy with lemon-fresh finish. You couldn't write a thesis on it, but the whistle-clean, tangy flavor makes it a pleasing everyday white	$	Drink when it's young and you may have found a real bargain
Entre-Deux-Mers	Bordeaux	France	Mainly Sauvignon-Sémillon, with a little Ugni Blanc and Muscadelle	Aromatic, with a whiff of freshly mown grass, and some ripe lemon and lime juice dancing on the tongue	$–$$$	Quality ranges wildly from this huge area of Bordeaux
Frascati	Lazio	Italy	Trebbiano and Malvasia	Dry, often bland – like a white wine spritzer minus the spritz. The best are more rounded, sometimes with a hint of Parma violet and some lime flavor	$	The Brits love Frascati, unaccountably, and drink more than the Italians
Fumé Blanc	Mainly California	United States	Sauvignon Blanc	Rich, oaked, often off-dry Sauvignon. Smokey hints from ageing in oak are reflected in name. Can be flabby, low in acid	$$	Wonderfully unfashionable style of wine that will impress at a 'Dynasty' theme party
Graves	Bordeaux	France	Sémillon and Sauvignon Blanc	The best are beautifully balanced – rich, barrel-fermented or aged, yet dry and fresh – a trade-off of fresh fruit and acidity, and round, creamy depths	$$–$$$	Name refers to the region, which has gravel soils. (Nothing to do with cemeteries)

NAME	REGION	COUNTRY	GRAPE	TASTE	PRICE	ANYTHING ELSE?
Liebfraumilch	Four regions of the Rhine-land	Germany	A blend, mainly Müller-Thurgau	Mild-mannered, off-dry, insipid, pathetic. Very occasionally a fresh, flowery, gently appley Lieb comes our way	$	Almost all made for export – the Germans aren't interested, because they're not stupid
Muscadet	Loire Valley	France	Melon de Bourgogne	Crisp, tart, lemony, sometimes with a light spritz. More serious examples have yeasty, biscuity, bready notes	$	Go for those labelled *sur lie* (on the lees) and the Sèvre-et-Maine appellation
Orvieto	Umbria	Italy	Trebbiano	Mostly dry, vaguely aromatic, some fresh, lemony fruit, and a hint of almond. There are some riper, more interesting wines knocking around	$–$$	Was originally a sweetish wine (*abboccato*), using some 'nobly rotten' grapes
Pouilly-Fumé	Loire Valley	France	Sauvignon Blanc	Bone dry and crisp, perfumed, with lemon-oil and mineral, flinty hints. Sniff out some gooseberry and elderflower here too	$$–$$$	Supposedly has a smoky flavor, like gunflint
Sancerre	Loire Valley	France	Sauvignon Blanc	Racy, dry white with pungent lemon, gooseberry and nettle character. Amazingly refreshing, summery stuff	$$–$$$	Quality varies, and styles range from delicate to richly aromatic and long-lived
Soave	Veneto	Italy	Mainly Garganega and Trebbiano	Often an uninspiring dry white with little discernible character. Track down a top producer, whose wines have perfumed lemon and almond character	$–$$	Chardonnay is being increasingly used in the blend leading to more rounded styles
Vinho Verde	Northwest	Portugal	Alvarinho, Loureiro, Trajadura and Pederna	Tart, racy, faintly spritzy, lightly floral. A hint of melon or lime juice, if you're lucky. Watery and boring, if you're not	$–$$	Drink as young as possible – freshness is everything here
Vouvray	Loire Valley	France	Chenin Blanc	Fresh green apples, hazelnuts, walnuts. Can be dry, and even rapier sharp when young, or softer and sweeter	$$	Try to resist the best wines until they take on richer tones of honey, bees-wax and yellow plums

light   medium-bodied   full/rich $–$$$ = bargain to bank-busting

White grape flavor tree

Chenin Blanc
Classic tasting notes are walnut, vomit and wet dog. Yum! Poor Chenin can be horrid, but the best Loire Valley examples are amazingly pure and snappy with intriguing notes of apple, honey and hay. Cape Chenin is much more humble, an easy-drinking party white.

Colombard
Bit of a yawn, and better used to make brandy, but Colombard is a mainstay of fresh, quaffable Southern French cheapies and some tasty, simple New World blends.

Viura aka Macabeo
Important in Spain, especially Rioja, where it makes fresh, lightish whites. Not thrilling.

Melon de Bourgogne
Sounds obscure but this is the racy, lemony grape behind Muscadet. Not exactly thrilling but often aged on yeast sediment for creamier depths.

Trebbiano aka Ugni Blanc
Mega-yawn. The bland grape variety behind much cheap Italian and French plonk. No discernible character and often turned into spirit.

Müller-Thurgau
More like Müller-Lite. Responsible for most of the sub-standard, dull Germanic whites that litter UK shopshelves. And you thought that was Riesling. Find some wet paint to watch instead.

Riesling
Much misunderstood, Riesling makes some of the finest wine in the world in Germany, Alsace, Austria, New Zealand and Australia. Its light, crisp, appley character is not fashionable, except among serious wine buffs. With age, picks up tremendous complexity and petrolly richness. Long over-due a revival.

Gewürztraminer
Number one stop on the vinous spice trail. Gewürz has an unmistakably exotic perfume of lychees, roses, peach-skin, ginger, lime and sweet cake spices. A superb partner for an oriental feast.

Muscat
Wine that tastes of grapes – whatever next! Crisp, dry Muscat is a refreshing summery treat.

Sauvignon Blanc
As Sancerre, a sophisticated bone dry white; in Bordeaux whites, helps create grassy, aromatic fresh wines; in New Zealand makes the earth move with its aromatic, ripe explosion of gooseberry fruit. Sauvignon can be cheap and cheerful, or pricey and rich. For all the pleasure it gives, still underrated.

Fumé Blanc
Want your Sauvignon oaked, off-dry and fat? No, we thought not.

Albariño

Fruity, aromatic, tangy grape that makes Spain's best white wines in the western Rias Baixas region.

Marsanne

Roussanne's blending partner in the Rhône, also making rich, weighty varietals in the South of France and Australia.

Viognier

Peachy, man. If you like New World Chardonnay, you'll love the full-on, sunny flavor of ripe Viognier, which can taste just like a fruit salad bursting with peaches and apricots. Reaches great heights in the Rhône Valley; also try Languedoc, Aussie and Californian examples.

Roussanne

One of the two grapes allowed into the Northern Rhône's white blend. Not fruity – more gingery. Rarely gets out on its own.

Chardonnay

Surely the most popular grape variety in the world, although some people hate the rich, toasty, creamy style. That's the oak, not the grape. Try a steely, crisp Chablis, a lighter Northern Italian Chardonnay or a New World wine that says 'unoaked' on the label (duh!). Aussie, Chilean and California Chardonnays tend towards richness, while New Zealand and South African wines can be a bit brisker. Eastern Europe and Vin de Pays d'Oc offer good value. Reaches its apex in complex, nutty, rounded white burgundies.

Sémillon

The generous, rounded curves of Sémillon pair up nicely with leaner, bonier Sauvignon in Bordeaux, while in the New World it is seen alone – rich, creamy, fruity and honeyed. Sensuous stuff.

Pinot Gris

In Alsace, a rich grape, making deeply colored, perfumed wines with smokey, spicy hints. In Italy, responsible for the more light-weight Pinot Grigio. Oregon and New Zealand interpretations well worth a try.

Pinot Blanc

An amiable creature, which makes soft, fruity stuff in Italy, Germany and Austria as well as more serious, food-friendly whites in Alsace.

light

medium-bodied

full/rich

suggested alternative

related

Rosé

Pink wine is sadly underrated. And here's why. There are so many weak, sour or sickly sweet rosés around that it's easy to give up after several nasty experiences. Then there's the persistent image problem. Despite the apparent rise of **New Man**, you rarely see a rugby team, or a businessman at a power lunch, tucking into a **bottle of pink** (unless you're in France or Spain). What a shame. Quaffing a fresh, young, **fruity** rosé, well-chilled and cracked open on a hot summer's day, is one of the most refreshing and delightful ways to enjoy wine that we can think of.

Think pink drink

It's time to sink some pink. The aroma of fine rosé is truly beguiling – a lovely compote of cherry, strawberry and rose-hip – the flavor has crisp, tangy acidity and a hint of cream. The golden rule is to guzzle it while it's young. That fragile, fresh fruit starts to fade about six months after bottling, and most light rosé has lost its bloom after a year. Rosé is made in one of three ways. Red grapes are crushed and their clear juice is left with the skins for a few hours to take on some color; for less color, the juice is run off and fermented on its own. Or, a drop or two of red wine is blended into white. Nothing wrong with that; they do it in Champagne.

Which are the rosiest of all?

France and Spain are the most important two countries for rosé. French rosés rely heavily on Cabernet Franc (in the Loire Valley), Merlot (in Bordeaux) and a trio of varieties, Syrah, Grenache and Cinsault, in the south. Generally, the further south you go, the riper the grapes, the richer the style. So Loire rosés are crisp and light, Bordeaux rosés are a tad fruitier, and southern ones have bolder, sunnier characters. The top French rosés are arguably the best in the world. The grottiest can be particularly vile.

Tapas tippling

Spain makes more reliable rosé (*rosado*), mainly from Grenache. From Rioja and Navarra it's particularly tasty stuff – lively, cherryish and tangy. It goes down extremely well with a plate of *jamòn* or a fresh prawn or two in a tapas bar. Elsewhere in Europe, Portugal has moved on from Mateus with a few drier styles, and Italy makes light and cheery Bardolino *rosato*.

New World order

The New World approach to rosé is to treat it as a light(ish) red, seen best in the full-on Grenache-based wines of Southern Australia, or the few fresh and aromatic Chilean and Argentinian examples, or the new wave of rich, deeply colored modern pinks from top California wineries.

Rosé style chart

NAME	REGION	COUNTRY	GRAPE	TASTE	PRICE	ANYTHING ELSE?
Bordeaux rosé	Bordeaux!	France	Mostly Merlot – occasionally Cab Sauv and Cabernet Franc	Bordeaux's rosés can be superb – fruity and fresh, strawberries and cream	$–$$	Just like Bordeaux's whites, much improved of late
Cabernet d'Anjou	Loire Valley	France	Cabernet Franc	Demi-sec (that's off-dry), juicy, good quality	$–$$	Considered more serious and classy than other Loire pinks
Provence	Deep South	France	Mainly Grenache and Cinsault	Too many are oxidised but others have ripe rose-hip character. Comes in funny bottles	$–$$	Traditional bottles are weirdly shaped, curving outwards in the middle like a bowling pin
Rosado	Rioja, Navarra, Somontano, Priorato	Spain	Usually Grenache, though check out others, such as local variety Bobal	Sunny, crisp, cherryish, mostly dry. Navarra rosé is packed with sweet, strawberryish fruit	$–$$	Under-rated outside Spain. Spanish *rosado* is deeply tempting, refreshing stuff
Rosato	Italy's Northeastern and Southern areas	Italy	Lagrein, Gaglioppo et al	Take your pick from bracing, tangy lighter *rosatos* (cool areas) and richer, riper ones (warmer climes)	$–$$	Italy calls its darker pinks '*chiaretto*' – from the word claret
Rosé d'Anjou	Loire Valley	France	Predominantly Grolleau	Not a lot. A simpering, tedious, even rather sickly, off-dry pink	$	A shame it pops up so much, as the Loire has better, less well-distributed rosés
Rosé de Loire	Loire Touraine, Anjou-Saumur	France	Cabernet Franc/ other Loire grapes	Always dry, usually lip-smackingly crisp and clean, if simple	$	Wave goodbye to sweet and cloying rosé hell!
Rosé de Riceys	Champagne	France	Pinot Noir	Serious rosé, with deep pink color and oodles of rich, raspberry fruit	$$	Very rare – go there to try it. Try the region's pink sparklers, too
Tavel	Rhône Valley	France	Grenache, Syrah, Cinsaut	Ripe, sun-kissed grapes produce rich rosé full of red-berry fruit, a hint of caramel and twist of spice	$$	Try Lirac too – these Rhône pinks are no wilting rosés
Vin gris, aka blush wines	California	United States	Several: Zinfandel and Grenache are popular	Sweetish, faintly spritzy, pale pink, deathly dull, utterly failing to set the world alight	$	Weedy white Zinfandel was first launched to appeal to America's white wine drinkers. Now Zin is more appreciated as a ruddy red, praise the lord

light   medium   rich $–$$$ = bargain to bank-busting

Rosé flavor bush

Eastern Europe
A few decent rosés, made from Cabernet or Merlot, have appeared from Hungary and Bulgaria. And they're good value.

England
Things have never looked better for the English rose... Made from Dornfelder and Pinot Noir, these crisp, well-balanced pinks are beginning to show great promise.

White Zinfandel
see California

Italy
Crack open a delicate, fresh *rosato* from northern Italy or a fruitier pink Cirò from the south.

Portugal
Drinking Mateus Rosé is taking the '70s revival a step too far. Try a new-wave, drier Portuguese pink instead – one or two are around.

France
Of the lighter Loire wines, Rosé d'Anjou can be dull and flimsy: other Loire labels are prettier in pink. Don't miss Bordeaux's medium-rich, fruity rosés, usually made from Merlot. Or Grenache- and Syrah-based pinks from Provence and the Southern Rhône, especially Tavel and Lirac. Some of these are rich and deeply-hued, tasting of ripe, sun-baked fruit.

 light

medium-bodied

full-bodied

Spain
A plate of *jamón*, a few prawns, and a frosty glass of finest fresh *rosado* – now you're talking! The brightest and best come from the Navarra, Rioja or Somontano regions, in the north of the country, and are usually produced from Grenache. Absolutely delicious. Salùd!

California
The off-dry wine known as White Zinfandel (actually pale pink) should make serious winemakers blush. Thank goodness for new West Coast rosés with a bit of oomph, especially those made from Syrah.

Chile
Not big on pink wine, but a few fresh, fruity Cabernet-based wines exist.

North Africa
Rare as hen's teeth, but a dribble of bright, modern pink wine is being exported from Algeria and Morocco to accompany trendy North African cuisine.

Australia
You wouldn't expect the Aussies to make wimpy, watery wine, now would you? They don't – they make big, ballsy, boisterous rosés, especially in South Australia. These wines, mostly from ultra-ripe Grenache and coming in at around 13% alcohol, are not to be messed with. Got that?

Argentina
Wash down your *empanadas* with one of the few rich and ripe rosés made in Mendoza.

Red wine

You may not think it, but there's loads you can learn about a red wine between the sound of the **cork** being pulled and the point where its **lingering** flavor slips down your gullet. There are clues a-plenty and you don't have to be Hercule Poirot to decipher them. What shade of red is it? Does it smell of red or black fruits? Why does it dry the front of your teeth? How does it **fill** (or fail to fill) every **nook** and **cranny** in your mouth? Work out the clues and you'll not only know what the wine tastes of, but why it tastes the way it does, and you'll enjoy it a lot more.

Ears, eyes, nose, throat...

Tasting may look silly, but the reasons for this apparently bizarre ritual of looking, smelling, swirling and spitting, are as good for red as they are for white wine. Ultimately, it's about bringing all your senses into play and using them to see not just what a red wine tastes like but why it tastes that way... and if you like it.

How is life on the edge?
Reds should be served at room temperature. What does that mean these days when most rooms are like saunas? There's nothing worse than tasting warm red wine, as heat blurs flavor, so try not to have the room too hot. Fill your glass about a third full and look at the color. It should be bright, never hazy. Now tilt it away from you and see what the color is like right at the edge of the wine (the rim). Young red wines are bright all the way to the edge, but as a red ages, that vibrant color fades and brown hues begin to appear. This is normal, but if a young wine looks brownish, prepare for an unpleasant experience. A red wine's color comes from the grape skin, so the thicker the skin, the deeper the color. Wine made from thick-skinned Cabernet or Syrah will be dark purple, while one from the thin-skinnned Pinot Noir will be lighter, more cherry-red.

Getting nosy
Now get your nose right in the glass and give it a good sniff. 70 percent of a wine's flavor is actually detected by the nose, so take your time. We're only too aware that there's a hell of a lot of pretentious guff written about what a wine smells like, but the fact remains that most wine doesn't smell of grapes! If a red wine smells of fruit (which it should) decide whether it is red or black fruit. Red fruits are raspberries, strawberries, red plums, cherries or redcurrants. Black fruits are blackcurrants, blackberrys, dark plums (damsons) and black cherries. A black fruit nose indicates a fuller-bodied wine, red suggests a lighter one, maybe with higher acidity. Now see what other aromas are hovering around. Mint can indicate Merlot or Cabernet; soot, pepper and toffee suggest Syrah; coconut matting and vanilla are an indication that American oak is being used; cinnamon and spice = French. Don't be scared of putting your own interpretation on the aroma, smell is a highly personal sense.

Frankie says... relax, don't swallow
Then take a sip and hold it in your mouth, chew it around and see how sweet or dry, full or light the wine is. Many of the aromas you noticed will be confirmed on the palate. Then check the 'feel' of the wine. Does it make the front of your teeth and the sides of your cheeks go dry? That's the tannin coming out to play. Tannins come from the skins, pips and stalks of the grape (and from wood). They form a leather skin on your cheeks – tanning them – and are a red wine's framework, acting as a preservative, helping it to age. Wines which are made to be drunk quickly shouldn't have huge amounts of tannin, but neither should the fruit be jammy or soupy. Balance is all-important.

Cabernet Sauvignon

The red king?

Cabernet and Chardonnay have a hegemony over every other variety, the red king and white queen gazing down from their thrones and scoffing at the lesser grapes desperately trying to ascend to their heights. Why Cabernet Sauvignon? For starters, Bordeaux is reckoned to make the finest, longest-lived red wines in the world and since they are made from Cabernet Sauvignon (there's also Merlot and Cabernet Franc in there, but let's not confuse matters) virtually every winemaker wants to try and make an equivalent wine.

Naughty naughty

There's another reason. Cab tastes great. There's something sweet, oozy and naughty about it. Stick your nose into a glass and out comes a heady, concentrated aroma of cassis, blackberries, brambles, briary fruits, all squished together along with mint and chocolate. Cabernet's greatest asset is the fact that, if made well, it can age superbly. Give the best some time and out comes marmite, game, leather and cedar/cigar box. That's a lot of flavors for one little grape. These days Cab winemakers fall into two camps: those who want to make wines their grandchildren will drink and others who want wine for instant gratification. Cabernet happily does both. It's a thick-skinned, small-berried grape, so has a high amount of skin (and pips) compared to the amount of juice. This means it not only gives a wine with lots of color, but high levels of tannin, perfectly matched to the French oak it matures best in.

The immigrant's song

It's the grape world's ideal immigrant: cheerfully packing its bags, putting down roots in any country and behaving impeccably well, sitting out in the sun getting a lovely blue sun tan. All this: great color, blackcurrant ripeness and an amenable nature has inevitably led it to be the world's favorite red variety. But the problem is 100 percent Cab wines can lack dimension. The last thing you want is a range of wines all tasting like blackcurrant jam, but increasingly that is what's being served up. The need for complexity is something the Bordelais realised early on. They planted Merlot and Cabernet Franc not only because Cabernet is a late ripener (at risk from cool autumn weather) but also because the wines are better with the extra layers of flavor these grapes provide. The Australians have done the same by blending in Shiraz, while Italians bring in Sangiovese. At the end of the day,

CELLAR, GLASS & PLATE

Storing: The greatest Bordeaux reds need years of cellaring before they start to open up, revealing perfumed aromas of cassis, game and cedar. New World examples tend to give more up-front fruit when young, but keep top-notch stuff for five years or more.

Serving: Decant top Cabs not only to separate any sediment which may have formed in long-cellared bottles, but also to aerate the wine so the heady aromas can swirl around your nose.

Matching with food: Those tannins are made to sit alongside red meat – and the rarer the better.

Who's the daddy?

Argentina

While Malbec will always be Argentina's trump card, better clones and vineyard management mean that Argentinean Cabernets are improving quickly. Look out for some good mid-priced Cabernet-Merlot-Malbec blends in the future.

Australia

The 'terra rossa' soil of the Coonawarra region has been the most highly prized land for Cabernet in Australia, giving long-lived wines with great structure and fruit-filled depth. Padthaway (equally big and strong) and Clare (more herbal and often blended with Malbec) are challenging hard, though the smart money is on Margaret River to give Coonawarra its greatest challenge. Margaret River Cabs (usually blended with Merlot and, increasingly, Malbec) have superb elegance and age well.

The Australians have also perfected the old Provençal blend of Cabernet and Syrah and given it a New World makeover. Their Cabernet-Shiraz blends are great, fruit-packed, mid-priced wines, where the soft, spicy sweet Shiraz plays against the currant and firmer structure of Cab.

Bulgaria

The country that brought the world of juicy, sweet blackcurrant Cabernet to the mass market (though much of it was actually originally South African wine shipped to eastern Europe in bulk!). The trouble is that Bulgaria hasn't yet (political instability, lack of finance) been able or willing to make the step up from mass-market juice to great wine.

California

Cabernet has been the red grape of choice in California since the late 1970s, when the industry started to establish itself as a producer of world-class wines. While in the early days it slavishly copied Bordeaux and ended up making tannic monsters, a Californian style is now emerging: richer, bolder and more concentrated than Bordeaux with firm but ripe tannin – a style that is made for earlier drinking.

One sip of a top Bordeaux and you know you're in the presence of something truly great – these wines are more than just beverages made from fruit...

That said, the latest trend in California is for wines which are as over the top in the fruit department as they used to be in tannin. These dense, fruit-packed, high alcohol monsters are gaining a cult following, but the finest examples of California Cabernet are more elegant and muted – wines from the Stags Leap district, and hillside sites in Napa and Sonoma. The mid-market wines tend to be high in fruit and low in complexity.

Chile

The classic modern Cabernet style – sweet juicy wines filled with cassis and blackberry – was pioneered by Chile. Maipo and Rapel are the best regions, with Rapel making the most interesting wine. Still great value and great to drink, the challenge for Chile is now to make wines which compete at the top level.

France

Bordeaux Not just the world's largest vineyard area, but home to some of its greatest wines, Bordeaux is where Cabernet Sauvignon rules with a haughty disdain. In simple terms, the left bank of the River Gironde (the Médoc and Graves) is Cabernet country, while on the right bank (Saint-Emilion and Pomerol) Merlot dominates the blend. The greatest *châteaux* are to be found in the communes of the Haut-Médoc (Pauillac, Margaux, Saint-Julien, Saint-Estèphe) and produce wines which have superb fragrance and a silky, elegant structure. One sip of a top Bordeaux and you know you're in the presence of something truly great – these wines are more than mere beverages made from fruit, they have entrancing layers of other aromas and flavors. Trouble is, you have to have a small fortune to afford them.

Don't expect the same hedonistic delights at the mid-price and cheapie level. With very few exceptions, these

The latest Californian trend is for wines which are as over the top in the fruit department as they used to be in tannin. These monsters are gaining a cult following...

wines are dilute and dreadful, an example of the parasitical relationship that befalls any great area – the inferior living in the reflected glory of the highest few.

Bergerac If you want reasonably-priced, richly-flavored Bordeaux-style French Cabernet go instead to Bergerac, a neighboring, but slightly warmer, area. There's a lot of money and young talent (much of it foreign) coming into a region which is really making it one to watch.

Lebanon
One of the great Cabernet-based wines comes from vineyards in the Bekaa Valley. Château Musar is a Cabernet-Cinsaut blend which is capable of amazing longevity. A more fruit-driven approach has been taken in recent years, but this is still one of the world's greatest wines.

New Zealand
Cabernet is a late ripener, which means it can struggle in cooler climates, taking on a herbaceous, green aroma. The Kiwis are persisting and, when the conditions are right, Waiheke Island and Hawke's Bay can make sensationally good examples.

South Africa
Though South Africa has made Cabernet-based wines for longer than any other New World country, problems with virus-affected vines have meant, in the past, the wines were often dry, dusty and green. New plant material is now going in and the changes have been remarkable. The next five years could see some world-class wines appearing.

Washington State
The high, dry, desert vineyards of the Pacific Northwest give intense Cabernets with notes of black cherry and tobacco. Though Merlot has been seen as the main variety, blends from areas like Walla Walla and Red Mountain are showing huge promise with Cabernet as well. Vast new vineyards of Cabernet mean that Washington State could soon be challenging Napa and Sonoma down south in California.

Pinot Noir

It smells of what?!

Let's face it, if you want to discover the most cussed, tricky, frustrating, finicky, gorgeous, sensuous red variety in the world you might as well stop here. Get Pinot Noir right and you'll have a red wine that surpasses every one of its rivals; get it wrong and you have either a thin, shrewish, acidic mess or an over-blown jammy dollop of fruit. When Pinot is cajoled into making a great wine, it leaves mere fruitiness behind, develops tannins that define silkiness, and has an ability to age that other reds would die for. Young Pinot smells of perfumed red fruits: strawberries, cherries, blueberries, along with a touch of earth. Give it time and out comes fungus, cooked cabbage, leather, the gunky mulch that's underfoot in a wood; smells that seem both out of place in a glass of wine, yet somehow lift it to another level. Polite folk talk of the 'aroma of the farmyard' but let's not beat about the silage, great Pinot smells of shit. And this is A Good Thing.

Pinot attention!

It's a fussy, thin-skinned grape which needs care and attention. Poorly made Cabernet may be boring but it's at least drinkable; even mediocre Pinot is horrible. And while Cabernet can grow anywhere, Pinot needs the right location, the right climate (not too hot, not too cold or damp), the right clones and, vitally, low yields, to stop it getting dilute. Now this is OK if you're in Burgundy, where you can draw on a thousand years of trial and error (though there's enough sub-standard wine to suggest not everyone does...), but in the rest of the world it's a different matter. While most non-Burgundian producers have managed sweet, jammy varietal wines, they struggle for the depth of character that defines truly great burgundy.

A case of Pinot envy?

It's the only grape that needs a certain kind of person to make it successfully. Pinot producers seem to flirt on the edge of insanity. They are obsessive by nature, the kind of people who enjoy putting their CDs in alphabetical order and debating endlessly whether Jimi Hendrix should be filed under rock, soul or jazz. Everyone thinks they have cracked it, they guard some secrets, borrow others, argue, hold conferences, fret and worry their lives away in the hope that, one day, it will all come right. It means that when buying Pinot you are often more likely to be disappointed than entranced, but please keep at it!

CELLAR, GLASS & PLATE

Storing: The key to Pinot Noir is knowing your producer. The *grands crus* can last for eons, *premier cru* and the best of the New World up to a decade. Standard Bourgogne and low-priced New World styles can be drunk from the word go.

Serving: Give it time to breathe: Pinot Noir benefits from interaction with air. Those aromas have cost you a lot of money, take time to appreciate them!

Food matching: Lighter examples are superb with salmon and firm-fleshed fish. Medium-bodied ones with duck. The biggest can cope with game.

Strawberry fields for ever

Australia

It was always going to take time for Australia to get to terms with Pinot. For starters, modern Australian viticulture was based in hot areas, exactly the conditions that Pinot Noir hates. Because not many of these older vineyards were in cool enough areas for the variety to prosper, early attempts were pretty disappointing. As new, cooler regions have come on stream so increasingly fine, fragrant examples have been made, though none have yet quite managed to capture the depth of flavor that sets red burgundy apart. Tasmania, Eden Valley, Lenswood, Yarra Valley and, surprisingly, Margaret River have led the way and remain the areas to watch.

Chile

Some low-priced Chilean Pinots are great – a fruity, cherry-berry mouthful with a bit of chocolate. Others simply don't come up to scratch. Choose with care – it's a case of trying to separate the shit-hot from the jammy shite.

France

Alsace In cool years Alsace Pinot is more like a rosé, in warmer years it picks up more color and berry fruitiness, but it never gets near the weight of burgundy. Chill it and drink it quickly. Great with fresh salmon...

Burgundy The region they all come to, in order to try and winkle out the arcane secrets of great Pinot, but there's probably more bad Pinot Noir made here than anywhere else. A case of too many people resting on their laurels. That said, the best are heady, sensual, silky and deep, without being heavy.

The Côte de Nuits is where Pinot reaches its greatest heights, from vineyards where the subtlest shift in soil and exposure seems to have a significant impact on the wine. These slopes are the temples for the highest acolytes of *terroir* (the site, soil, sun, rain etc of the location where the grapes are grown). Now you may be cynical about the concept, but we've both tasted wines made in the same way but which came from different soils no more than a few feet apart. They tasted quite different. Because Burgundy has been sub-divided into minuscule plots of land, winemakers have been able to observe the tiny nuances of difference and exploit them. Don't let that convince you that good *terroir* equals good wine. Ultimately quality is down to how talented the winemaker is, not what sort of dirt he grows his vines on.

Low yielding vines, fermenting in wood, ageing in (mostly) old barrels, are enough to give anyone Pinot-envy. Remember, though, names such as Gevrey-Chambertin and Nuits-Saint-Georges aren't a guarantee of quality. Get to know your supplier, get to know your producer and be prepared to spend money! The greatest burgundies are made in small quantities and ain't cheap.

Champagne Pinot is a vital ingredient in the best Champagnes, giving them a red berry fruit lift.

Loire At one time there was more red than white made in areas like Sancerre. These days you can find the occasional light, often grassy, example but, like Alsace, either treat it like a rosé, or stick to white.

New Zealand

The coolest climate in the New World not surprisingly produces some of its finest Pinots. They are occasionally vegetal but have now moved away from the light strawberry jam of the past and are becoming wines with

Winemakers have been able to observe tiny nuances of difference and exploit them. But don't let that convince you that good terroir equals good wine!

fragrance but good depth. Martinborough, Marlborough and Central Otago are New Zealand's regions to watch.

Romania

Full-on lush Pinot for everyday drinking. Good value as well.

South Africa

A small but dedicated band of obsessives, based on the coast at Walker Bay, have been persevering

with Pinot for nearly 20 years and are at last beginning to hit their straps – especially now that they have planted Burgundian clones instead of the Swiss sparkling wine clones they were initially sold. There's been a re-examination of the vineyard, a scaling down of new wood in the cellars and increasingly impressive results. Even they agree that the best areas for Pinot in the country may not have been discovered yet.

USA

California Early indications suggested that Carneros may be the best place for Pinot in California, but the wines have never quite achieved the depth of character that great Pinot needs. Significantly better wines are coming from the cool-climate sites in Santa Barbara. The message is clear: Go south young man!

North to Oregon… An Oregonian Pinot Noir shocked the world by beating the French hands down in a blind tasting in the 1980s. Since then, the state's performance has been patchy, but a handful of top producers are making silky, long-lived wines with fleshy, strawberry and plum weight.

Merlot

Isn't Merlot a bit like Cabernet?

Yes, and no. It's a totally separate grape, capable of making generously fruity, divinely smooth, sweetly ripe reds all on its own. More famously, it is paired up with Cabernet Sauvignon in blends (the winemakers don't always tell you it's there). The idea is that the plump, fleshy Merlot fruit fills out the leaner, more tannic Cabernet.

A marriage made in heaven?

Most of the time. Look at the great clarets (red Bordeaux). Merlot is a superb blending grape, which quietly gives more pleasure than many wine drinkers realize, as its name rarely appears on the label of classic French *cuvées*. That said, varietal Merlot has become hugely fashionable in the New World of late, producing modern, intensely fruity reds in California and Chile in particular. Think ripe, juicy purple plums wrapped in a layer of chocolate. You won't find many people who dislike New World Merlot. It's easy-going, medium-bodied stuff, generally of a high standard, and food-friendly to boot. For the most serious Merlot, try the concentrated, supple wines of Saint-Emilion and Pomerol in Bordeaux; they may contain other grapes, but they rely much more heavily on Merlot fruit than any other.

Sounds pricey...

Not necessarily. Chilean Merlot can be good value, and nowadays it's extremely easy to get hold of. There are some affordable, tasty Merlots knocking about from Southwest France, Northern Italy and Eastern Europe, too. If you are exploring the grape for the first time, however, start with the luscious South American wines – they're a bargain. And be sure to avoid cheap, thin, dilute clarets – these are where Merlot is at its most miserable.

CELLAR, GLASS & PLATE

Storing: Light Merlots need drinking up within a year. Then again, the very richest, oak-aged single varietals and blends (especially tight-knit Left Bank clarets) can take a long time to unfurl and reveal their soft center. The Merlot-based wines from Pomerol and Saint-Emilion are relatively approachable when young – for claret – but even more seductive after eight to ten years bottle age.

Serving: At room temperature

Matching with food: The most serious wines go with roast beef, beef stews, steak and kidney pie, roast game birds.

Plump plums

Australia

Australian winemakers prefer blending Cabernet with Shiraz rather than Merlot, although there are one or two excellent, full-bodied exceptions. Rarely appears alone Down Under.

Eastern Europe

If you want decent Merlot or Cab-Merlot with a soothing price tag, you could do worse than trying a fruity Bulgarian, Romanian or Hungarian label.

France

There's more Merlot than any other grape in Bordeaux. It may be less 'starry' than Cabernet Sauvignon, but Merlot plays a major role alongside Cab in creating Bordeaux reds both fine and feeble. From the specific Bordeaux regions of Saint-Emilion and Pomerol, it dominates the blend, making majestic wines with fulsome, plummy fruit and well-rounded tannins – in fact some of the world's greatest reds. The South (Bergerac, Languedoc-Roussillon) provides an ocean of red made with Merlot or Merlot blends. Quality of these wines ranges widely.

Italy

Soft, light Merlots and blends with Cabernet are mainly made in the North, particularly the northeast. Tread carefully around the more dilute, grassy wines and track down the few serious, well-structured examples.

New Zealand

The latest Merlots and Cab-Merlots to emerge from the warmer regions (Hawke's Bay, Waiheke Island), show that Merlot has come into its own in New Zealand. Grassy herbaceous flavors are being replaced by signs of real ripeness – lush, red berry character and good structure.

South Africa

Cape Merlots and Merlot blends (with Cab and Shiraz) from the Stellenbosch, Paarl and, lately, Malmesbury regions, can be rich and classy, with firm, often oaky tannins.

South America

Of all the mid-priced reds in the world, Chilean Merlot has to rank as among the best value. The wines are generally fruit-packed, modern and juicy, and more smokey, oak-aged Chileans exist too. But Chilean Merlot is not all it often appears to be. A high proportion has been found to be another variety, Carmenère. In the future the two will be labelled more accurately. Some promising Merlot is produced in the Mendoza region of Argentina too.

USA

California's winemakers are behind impressively concentrated, well-proportioned, ripe Merlots, arguably the best in the New World. They also produce their fair share of weak and jammy wines, and some over-oaked and over-priced ones too. Washington State's Columbia region and Long Island in New York State both turn out some good-quality Merlots.

Syrah/Shiraz

Why are they lumped together?

Ah, but they're one and the same grape. It's called Syrah in France and Shiraz in Australia. Some other countries use Shiraz and some use Syrah, so expect to see either on a label. Or nothing at all: in the Rhône Valley, where the top Syrahs are made, producers don't put any grape variety on the label, which is fairly typical French practice. For the record, Syrah got its second name Down Under when vines were taken to Australia from the South of France under the name 'Scyras'. Eventually it was corrupted to Shiraz, which sounds less like a Soviet space station.

Did it catch on in Australia then?

Just a bit. Shiraz was Australia's trusty workhorse grape for over a century, producing oceans of old-fashioned fortified wines and 'Dry Reds' until as recently as the 1970s. Now it is taken much more seriously – perhaps more seriously than any other grape in the country – and is used to create rich, smooth, powerful reds in several regions of Oz. Ancient gnarled vines, sometimes over a century old, play a large part in today's concentrated, blockbuster style. Aussie Shiraz is also blended very successfully with Cabernet. From France, Syrah gives intense, smokey,

peppery reds in the Northern Rhône, and makes an invaluable contribution to sun-baked, richly alcoholic Southern Rhône reds (such as Châteauneuf-du-Pape). Although Syrah/Shiraz is mainly found in France and Australia, it has caught on elsewhere, and today ranks as something rather fashionable – not bad for a former workhorse. It's popular in South Africa and California in particular, and plenty of others are having a stab too. These pioneers are nicknamed the Rhône Rangers.

Why haven't you said 'fruity' yet?

Well spotted. It's because reds (as opposed to rosés) made from Syrah/Shiraz are not overtly fruity – they lack the bright primary fruit flavors of Cabernet or Merlot. Instead, they offer unusual nuances of spice, toffee, herbs, smoke, cream, leather, pepper. That said, ripe young New World wines can be thick with blackcurrant, and unripe, cheap French Syrah has a mundane, rather acidic, red-berry character.

Did someone say 'sweaty saddles'?

A classic, if decidedly weird, tasting note for Hunter Valley Shiraz. Can't say we've ever spotted it, but then we don't go round sniffing warm saddles. A certain whiff of leather and stable does sometimes waft up from the glass – it's more appealing than it sounds.

CELLAR, GLASS & PLATE

Storing: Rich, concentrated wines (from any region) last for years and years – try approaching them after ten. Drink lighter, fruitier wines within a year, or perhaps two.

Serving: Serve at room temperature.

Matching with food: An extremely useful Sunday roast wine. Peppery Northern Rhône reds are ace with roast game, beef or pork, while mid-weight Aussie Shiraz is perfect for roast turkey or goose. Lighter Rhône blends (Côtes-du-Rhône) are a better match with roast chicken. All are good partners for strong, hard cheeses.

Spicing it up around the world

Argentina

Syrah (that's what they usually call it) from the Mendoza region is exciting stuff – ripe, smooth and spicy. This grape variety holds great promise for Argentinian producers, who already know a thing or two about rich, supple reds after making so much delicious Malbec.

Australia

Australia's most famous wine, Penfold's Grange, is always made from Shiraz grapes. Its dark, wonderfully concentrated, long-lived style has been copied by many top producers, but the fact is that no two Australian Shirazes taste the same. Grange is mainly made from Barossa grapes – this hot, dry valley in South Australia makes immense, but smooth, ripe reds out of old-vine fruit. They're the gentle giants of the wine world.

The Hunter Valley has moved away from the classic earthy, leathery styles it was once renowned for, and now makes somewhat cleaner Shiraz. Western Australian styles can be more Rhône-like and McLaren Vale wines are dominated by creamy chocolate. But then you'll probably have a different interpretation of the regional characteristics

when you taste them yourself. One thing is certain, Aussie Shiraz is a fascinating, satisfying, heavyweight style of red wine. It's reliable too – the medium and top-priced wines are rarely duds. That goes for the more expensive Shiraz and Cabernet Sauvignon blends too.

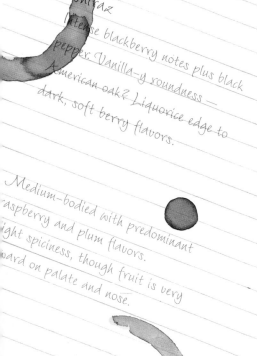

Shiraz
(Intense blackberry notes plus black
pepper. Vanilla-y roundness —
American oak? Liquorice edge to
dark, soft berry flavors.

Medium-bodied with predominant
raspberry and plum flavors.
light spiciness, though fruit is very
ward on palate and nose.

nt, almost
ry and
ft-black
s.

The cheapest, lighter reds made from Shiraz are soft, sunny, easy-drinking wines, great for barbecues. But when it comes down to it, the Australian version of Syrah is, and always will be, a big wine. Never too big to sparkle, though. (See Sparkling Reds, page 78.)

Chile

Several impressive Chilean Syrahs exist. Promising, but there are few vineyards planted at the time of writing. Watch this space.

France

Northern Rhône The mighty reds are deeply colored, densely flavored and defiantly long-lived. In fact, they're well-loved Syrah classics. Wines made in the Côte-Rôtie are huge, growling monsters while young, although

Wines made in Côte-Rôtie are huge, growling monsters while young, although they have a strangely elegant perfume owing to a bit of white Viognier.

they can have a strangely elegant perfume owing to a bit of white Viognier in the blend. Hermitage also takes several years to open up – try storing it away for a decade – and mellow out, while its cousin Crozes-Hermitage can be smoother, but still

powerful. Cornas is another source of fine, rich Syrah, and Saint-Joseph, although not quite as reliable as its neighbours, can often provide a decent bargain.

Southern Rhône Here Syrah is rarely used alone, but blended with a cocktail of other black grapes (Grenache and Mourvèdre are the most important ones), to make spicy, ripe wines from Châteauneuf-du-Pape (where it's one of up to 13 grapes used), Gigondas, Lirac, Vacqueyras and others. The less expensive Côtes du Rhône-Villages wines can be great value. Simple Côtes du Rhône ranges widely in quality, and is often, unfortunately, rather jammy and weak.

South of France Syrah makes a lot of tasty, modern, ripe *vin de pays* red, either on its own or as part of a blend of varieties.

Italy

A few of the more progressive Italian winemakers are keen on Syrah – it pops up in Tuscany, on its own and blended in with the local staple Sangiovese. It has even cropped up in the mix for Valpolicella up in the Veneto, and appears again in Sicily, where it certainly gets all the sun-kissing it needs.

h

New Zealand

Not the first grape to spring to mind when you think of New Zealand, as Syrah requires a hot sun, but some surprisingly successful wines are made in the North Island, especially in the warm Hawke's Bay region. More plantings of Syrah are set to come on stream in the Land of the Long White Cloud in the next few years.

South Africa

There is plenty of South African Shiraz which tastes clumsy, over-alcoholic and baked but, then again, some more refined wines are available which have lovely plummy depths and good firm structure. Pick your producer with care. It's often blended with Cabernet Sauvignon and, less frequently, with Merlot and Pinotage.

Uruguay

Uruguayan Syrah sounds utterly obscure, we know. But alongside and (sometimes blended with) the national grape Tannat, which is also dark and leathery, Syrah is tipped as a variety likely to help put this country on the wine-producing map.

USA

Syrah in the States grew very fashionable in California throughout the late 1980s and 1990s, where 'Rhône Rangers' (winemakers whose passion for Rhône grapes led to their nickname) such as Randall Grahm of Bonny Doon set about making Syrah and Syrah blends with rich fruit but impressive elegance. We've tasted top-notch Syrah from Washington State as well.

Grenache

The Big Yin

There isn't another red variety that brings such wild, untamed exuberance to the world of wine as Grenache. It's a Billy Connolly among grapes: big, bold and crude but somehow friendly, loveable and appealing. No surprise that it's the second most widely-planted vine on the planet.

The reign of Spain

These days, Grenache is seen as a southern French variety, at home on the southern Rhône delta, Roussillon and along the Mediterranean coast. In fact, like Mourvèdre, it was originally from Spain and spread into France as the kingdom of Aragon expanded its borders, which seems a very civilised way to take over another country. Yup, Garnacha is Grenache.

So why isn't it famous?

It's been planted in the 'wrong' places. Grenache has been seen as a blender, with none of the finesse of Bordeaux or Burgundian varieties. It's another Mediterranean grape that's been sneered at by the wine snobs who believed that only Cabernet, Merlot and Pinot Noir were capable of making top-quality wine – remember Syrah has only recently been accepted into the premier league.

There's another problem. Get low-yielding, dry-farmed old Grenache vines and you have a wine that's packed full of sweet, rich, chocolatey, spicy, black-fruited flavors. Trouble is, it's been planted in areas where producers either wanted high-yielding vines for table wine

CELLAR, GLASS & PLATE

Storing: Grenache is low in tannin and filled with fruit so it's best to drink it within a year or two of bottling. The exceptions are the wines from Priorat: they need time... lots of it (they can last for decades).

Serving: In as big a glass as you have and at room temperature.

Matching with food: Game, sausages and gravy, barbie foods, kangaroo and ostrich. You get the idea – it's not a hugely complex wine but a fun one.

or super-ripe raisins for fortified production. Result? Most Grenache/Garnacha is thin in fruit, light in color, and, unfortunately, weedy in flavor.

Moving on up
Recently there's been a revival. The Rhône has become hip, big flavors are in, and now quality winemakers using the simple formula of old vines, no irrigation, low yields and careful handling are showing that Grenache can make exuberant, exciting wines. They may not last as long as Syrah but boy, are they a fun mouthful!

More grunt than a grizzly

Australia
One reason Grenache was planted Down Under was for 'port', but as that market collapsed winemakers began pouring on the water and turned it into a bland, boring blender. After all, Oz is now set up for mechanical-harvested, irrigated vineyards, not dry-farmed, bush-trained vines. It's being taken seriously in the Barossa, though some winemakers appear to have forgotten that they're not making so-called 'port' any more and Grenache doesn't have to be 16% ABV, thick as treacle and with an instant headache in the bottle.

France
Though Grenache has been behind some of the greatest wines from Châteauneuf-du-Pape and is the main player in France's best *vins doux naturels* (sweet wines) – Banyuls and Maury – it has mostly been anonymously blended away in very *ordinaire* wine. Now, with the southern quality renaissance gathering pace, expect to see it moving onto center stage.

Italy
As Cannonau, Grenache is behind the best wines coming from Sardinia. Wild, earthy stuff.

Spain
Calatayud A forgotten, dry, high plateau region that's filled with old bush vine Garnacha; a recipe for success go-ahead co-ops are exploiting.

Navarra Until recently, Garnacha was for *rosado*, Tempranillo and Cab for reds. Now old vine red wines are being made, but it'll be a long slog.

Priorat/Tarragona These remote mountain vineyards give intensely flavored, solidly structured red wines with massive extract and deep fruitiness. Priorat is pricey, Tarragona more wallet-friendly. Both are making the most exciting wines in Spain – and Garnacha is the main player.

Rioja Here Garnacha is mainly used to give volume and juicy weight to Tempranillo.

USA
Widely planted, but mainly in the flat, hot, irrigated Central Valley vineyards in California. Grenache was behind the jug and fortified wines drunk by bums and hobos. Now that Syrah has finally been given a green light, Grenache's time may be coming. Good things could happen.

Sangiovese

Don't tell me, it's Italian...

And how. Sangiovese is so rooted in the Italian soil that its name means 'Blood of Jove'. Planted across the country, it reaches its greatest heights in Tuscany where it's the basis for Brunello di Montalcino, Vino Nobile di Montalcino and Chianti. Wine in raffia flasks? No thanks. Think again. The days of the straw *fiasco* (never was a name so appropriate) are long gone. Still, it's worth dwelling on the memories of thin, acidic, abrasive red wine because they demonstrate what can happen if you don't get Sangiovese under control. It's a slow ripener, which is fine in hot years, but in cool, damp

the wrong grape clones and then pushing yields up as high as they possibly could.

Make mine a Merlot then...

Hang on a minute. There's been a turnaround in Tuscany. The Italians are paying attention. The right clones are going in, yields have come down, small barrels are being used, Cabernet is being blended in to fill Sangiovese out. The task is to beef up this grape without losing its cherry, red plum and coffee and tobacco, and tame its tannins and acidity without losing its signature of fresh tartness – which, after all, is what makes it such a great food wine. It's time to rediscover it.

> ## CELLAR, GLASS & PLATE
>
> **Storing:** Cheap Chianti can be drunk instantly, but riserva bottlings and top IGT, and vini di tavola need time. Give 'em five years or more.
>
> **Serving:** Decant riserva wines
>
> **Matching with food:** Meats: roast pork, lamb, grilled steak, spag bol, melanzane parmigiana (that's aubergines, mozzarella, basil and tomato). Game birds are best of all.

The days of the straw fiasco *(never was a name so appropriate) are long gone. Still, it's worth dwelling on the memories...*

conditions acid and tannin rule the roost. Not exactly the blood of a god.... Sangiovese vines are also vigorous, and the higher they're allowed to yield, the lighter the color and more acidic the grapes will be. Much of that astringent Chianti that you didn't enjoy in your local *trattoria* was the product of winemakers planting

What about the rest of the world?

Sangiovese makes table wine in Argentina and although immigrants took it to California and Australia years ago, the French hegemony of the world's wine has meant Italian varietals have been seen as second best. There are some 'Super-Napans' emerging from California, but nothing earth-shaking yet.

Tempranillo

Who is that masked grape?

Grape varieties change names occasionally, but none can top Tempranillo. This variety moves across Spain and the Iberian peninsula like some vinous secret agent traveling under many different aliases. It's a shape shifter as well, changing its character as it goes, hiding its personality beneath wood, slipping into the shadows behind other grape varieties.

Some believe it's a distant relation of Pinot Noir, and certainly in Rioja it can show some chocolate-coated strawberry notes, though the chocolate may come from Garnacha. Riojan producers have long known it works well with American oak – almost too well as it seems only too willing to let the vanilla from the wood dominate. In Navarra it has a softer plummier flavor, though that may be down to the Cabernet

Some believe it's a distant relation of Pinot Noir, but as Cencibel in Valdepeñas and La Mancha, it appropriately enough makes sensible 'Man at C&A' type wines...

Sauvignon it's blended with. Known as Ull de Llebre (eye of the hare) in Catalonia, it's a worthy but unexciting blender, while in La Mancha and Valdepeñas as Cencibel, it appropriately enough makes sensible, 'Man at C&A' type wines. Because Tempranillo flowers late and ripens early, it misses the worst of the spring and autumn frosts in Ribera del Duero and Toro (where it's called Tinto Fino and Tinto de Toro and produces black-hearted, flavorsome wines that are at the heart of the Spanish red renaissance. If you want food to match with it , go for lamb.

We've both come back from Spanish trips with lamb-stuffed buttocks thanks to being served it four times a day, seven days a week, washed down with Tempranillo of course.

And the next mission will be?

This name-changing business isn't just restricted to Spain. In Portugal, where it's used to make port in the Douro Valley, Tempranillo is known as Tinta Roriz, and it's now also making a name for itself (as Aragonez) in lush wines from the Alentejo. Argentinians call it Tempranilla, and haven't rated it that highly, though that's all changing.

More red grapes

They think it's all over...

If shelf presence is anything to go by, then you would be forgiven for thinking that there were no red grape varieties worth drinking other than Cabernet Sauvignon, Merlot... oh, and maybe perhaps Shiraz. These three varieties dominate the offerings in liquor stores and restaurants so effectively that you are given the mistaken impression the world's other red grapes are inferior both in terms of flavor and quality.

But they're plain wrong!

Needless to say this just isn't true. The world is full of many other magnificent red grapes. Some are hidden away in blends, offering understated support to big guns like Cabernet Sauvignon; others lurk behind appellations which forbid the use of a grape's name on the label (yes, you guessed it, it's the French wines that are mostly guilty here). Whatever the reason for their anonymity (or lack of wider recognition) these grapes are well worth discovering for their highly individual characters and flavors. Here's the best of the rest – and a few of them are superstars . Try 'em, you may be surprised.

The support team

Aglianico

It's the bitter edge to the perfumed scent of cloves and plums that gives Aglianico away. Only Italian red grapes have this savory/sweet character. At home around the Campanian town of Taurasi and on the slopes of Mont Vulture in Basilicata, there's an almost decadent quality to its fruit that gives wines which are rich, wild and lush.

Baga

In Portuguese 'Baga' means 'berry' which is a pretty accurate description of this small, thick-skinned, sun-gnarled little blue-coated peasant of a grape. It can be a tough little baga, and as tannic as a pair of old work boots, but pick it at the right time and work it gently in the winery to prevent those tannins getting grip and it gives wines with perfume, weight and black-fruited power. At its best in Bairrada but being grown (and blended) across the country.

Barbera

This might be Italy's second-biggest variety, but somehow it's seen as a bit of an also-ran. A late ripener, it can be mouth-hurtingly tart (even the best examples have this fresh bite on the finish) but with care – low yields and a short time in new barrels – it can make wines with lovely sweet, plum and cherry concentration. It can age, but Barbera is one of those wines that's meant to be opened, poured and loved.

Cabernet Franc

Cab Franc suffers from little brother syndrome. While Cabernet Sauvignon is the popular sports jock who always gets the girl, his brother Franc gets on with his work and is always there to give Sauvignon a bit of support when he needs it, which is more often than many realise. He also does the same with Merlot, particularly in

Saint-Emilion and Pomerol. Perfume is Cab Franc's defining trait and even a drop can lift a blend. It's fragrant, but in a dusty, bosky, woodland kind of way: pencil shavings, fresh earth, grass, violets, raspberries – it can even stray into Black Forest gateau territory with aromas of black cherry and chocolate. Mostly seen in blends, but some great single varietals are made in South Africa and the Loire – prepare to be beguiled by Bourgueil.

Corvina

Sounds like a grape from a Ford factory, but is actually the main red variety behind Valpolicella. Forget the wishy-washy style of the past and go for wines labelled *classico, ripasso, recioto* and *amarone*. Think fresh black cherries, think perfume, but please re-think Valpol.

Dolcetto

Sweeter and lighter than Barbera, Dolcetto makes gorgeous, drink-me-now, purple, fruit-packed wine that's like biting into a tart red plum.

Gamay

Gamay is Beaujolais, all about sweet shops, strawberry ice lollies, juicy red fruits and lightly chilled bottles of wine that make people smile. Don't go for the ghastly marketing con of Nouveau but the single village ('*cru*') wines with fragrance and juice-filled depth.

Malbec

Originally from Cahors and a minor blending grape in Bordeaux, Malbec was one of the huddled masses that emmigrated to Argentina and in the high desert of Mendoza it blossomed into a wanton, black-haired sultry temptress, full of silky dark fruit.. Swoon at its power.

Mourvèdre

Small, sweet and thick-skinned, this is a grape that loves heat and can give rich, dark-colored wines filled with blackberries and tanned animal hide (this is good!). Under the monicker of Monastrell it's behind dark-fruited reds from Jumilla in southern Spain, as Mourvèdre it's the main grape of Bandol, and as Mataro behind new Rhône-esque blends from Oz. It can be a little hollow, so it needs support – Grenache/Garnacha or Syrah/Shiraz are its ideal *compadres*.

Nebbiolo

There are wine lovers who swear that this enigmatic northern Italian variety, the grape behind Barolo and Barbaresco, is the greatest red wine grape in the world. It's also one of the most tricky for the wine maker to use. Incredibly late ripening (a drawback in fog-shrouded Piedmont where autumn arrives suddenly), high in tannins and acid, few red grapes

have an aroma like it. Don't expect jammy super-ripe fruit, this is a smell which is heady, savory and strangely non-wine like: a haunting aroma of rose petals, liquorice and freshly caulked boats, a touch of roasting tins and truffles. Get that fruit in between the tannin/ acid sandwich and it's a long-lived, light colored masterpiece. Sadly, Nebbiolo's awkward nature means few other regions have mastered it.

Nero d'Avola

Never heard of it? You will soon. It's is the Syrah of Sicily, making wonderfully perfumed, dark, smooth reds that not only can be aged in barrique, but positively love being surrounded by wood. When Sicily went white a few years back, much old vine Nero was pulled up, but new quality-conscious producers who are hauling this huge island into the brave new world of high-quality, fruit-packed wine have persevered with it. Wonderful blended with Syrah, Cabernet or Merlot it can also stand on its own two feet. The Sicilian revival starts here!

Zin can ripen unevenly, so growers have to keep it hanging on the vine, then BANG! it's overripe and you're making wine with the same alcohol level as port...

Negroamaro

Many southern Italian winemakers think that Negroamaro rather than Primitivo is the variety to watch. It has a powerful, black cherry aroma with that bitter twist on the finish that is typically Italian. Look for Salice Salentino or Copertino. If you've already fallen for the Gothic delights of Amarone, try dried-grape Negroamaro which tastes like it's been squeezed from sweet black rock.

Pinotage

South Africa's very own red variety is a cross between Pinot Noir and Cinsault. It can be estery (ie, it smells of nail polish and banana peel) but

handled well in vineyard and winery, it's pruney, grunty and deep. OK, it might not make the finest wine in the world but it's a real rustic romp.

Primitivo

The name says it all. Primitivo is filled with primal, ancient flavors. Densely structured with a darkly wild fruitiness, it's thought to be the Italian ancestor of Zinfandel and shares that grape's tendency for soupy alcoholic excess.

Touriga Nacional

For years the core of the finest ports, the deeply colored Touriga Nacional with its headily perfumed concentration and firm tannins is now seen as Portugal's top red variety and is being planted across the country.

Zinfandel

Forget hideous 'White Zin', here we're talking about the real stuff: a red wine that can smell of rosemary, peach, mulberry, earth and cranberry. Zin can ripen unevenly, so growers have to keep it hanging on the vine, then BANG! it's overripe and you're making wine with the same alcohol level as port. Western Australia has a decent one and the South Africans are playing with it, but its home is firmly in the old vine plantings of California.

Red wine styles

NAME	REGION	COUNTRY	GRAPE	TASTE	PRICE	ANYTHING ELSE?
Bairrada	er, Bairrada	Portugal	Baga	Dense, darkly-fruited, perfumed. A meaty mouthful	$–$$	A region to watch for serious new wave reds
Barolo and Barbaresco	Piedmont	Italy	Nebbiolo	Bad Barolo can be viciously tannic and acidic. The greatest smell of game, truffles, roses and tar. Barbaresco is a (slightly) lighter neighbour	$$–$$$	At its best, Italy's greatest red. A 'modern' winemaking approach has transformed the region
Beaujolais	Burgundy	France	Gamay	The juiciest, reddest fruits you've ever squeezed into your mouth – and tomato soup and banana. Obscenely mouth-watering	$–$$	Forget Nouveau, stick to the crus such as Fleurie, Morgon, Saint-Amour and Moulin-à-Vent
Bergerac Rouge	Dordogne	France	Cab Sauvignon and Merlot	Rich, full-bodied reds with some blackcurrant aromas	$–$$	Not as glamorous or as famous as Bordeaux, but infinitely more reliable and at a decent price
Bourgogne	Burgundy	France	Pinot Noir	At its best, silky blueberries, raspberries and a whiff of farmyard manure. At its worst, mean and acidic	$$–$$$	Burgundy is frustrating, yet wonderful. Pick your supplier carefully and save your pennies
Cahors	Midi-Pyrenees	France	Malbec	The best have an aroma of wild black berry fruits	$$	Slowly getting better
Châteauneuf-du-Pape	Rhône Valley	France	Grenache (plus another 12 permitted!)	Spicy, rich and dense, or boring and jammy, or tannic. Take your pick	$$–$$$	Famous (but overrated) area now taking stock and coming up with better, denser wines
Chianti	Tuscany	Italy	Sangiovese (plus Cab Sauvignon)	Black or morello cherries, and a bitter twist on the finish (which can be refreshing or unbalancing)	$–$$$	The cradle of Italy's wine renaissance. No straw flasks, Chianti is serious, seductive stuff
Claret/ Bordeaux Rouge	Bordeaux	France	Cab Sauvignon, Merlot and Cab Franc	Everything from sublime cassis, currant and cigar boxes to thin red fruit-free dross	$–$$$	Avoid wines with just 'claret' on the label
Côte-Rôtie	Rhône Valley	France	Syrah	Intensely-flavored, sexy wines filled with soot, savory black fruit and pepper	$$$	Buy it and then sit on it for a few years. This is a wine that needs time

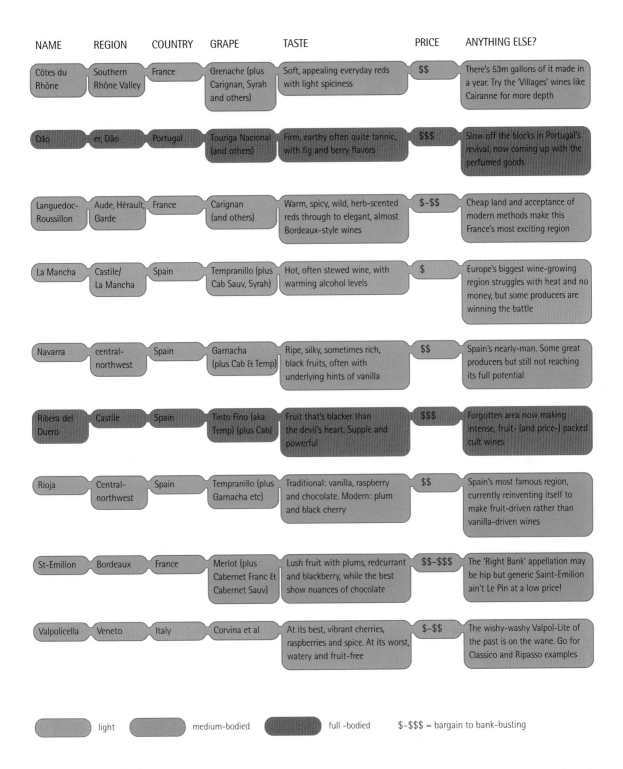

NAME	REGION	COUNTRY	GRAPE	TASTE	PRICE	ANYTHING ELSE?
Côtes du Rhône	Southern Rhône Valley	France	Grenache (plus Carignan, Syrah and others)	Soft, appealing everyday reds with light spiciness	$$	There's 53m gallons of it made in a year. Try the 'Villages' wines like Cairanne for more depth
Dâo	er, Dâo	Portugal	Touriga Nacional (and others)	Firm, earthy often quite tannic, with fig and berry flavors	$$$	Slow off the blocks in Portugal's revival, now coming up with the perfumed goods
Languedoc-Roussillon	Aude, Hérault, Garde	France	Carignan (and others)	Warm, spicy, wild, herb-scented reds through to elegant, almost Bordeaux-style wines	$-$$	Cheap land and acceptance of modern methods make this France's most exciting region
La Mancha	Castile/ La Mancha	Spain	Tempranillo (plus Cab Sauv, Syrah)	Hot, often stewed wine, with warming alcohol levels	$	Europe's biggest wine-growing region struggles with heat and no money, but some producers are winning the battle
Navarra	central-northwest	Spain	Garnacha (plus Cab & Temp)	Ripe, silky, sometimes rich, black fruits, often with underlying hints of vanilla	$$	Spain's nearly-man. Some great producers but still not reaching its full potential
Ribera del Duero	Castile	Spain	Tinto Fino (aka Temp) (plus Cab)	Fruit that's blacker than the devil's heart. Supple and powerful	$$$	Forgotten area now making intense, fruit- (and price-) packed cult wines
Rioja	Central-northwest	Spain	Tempranillo (plus Garnacha etc)	Traditional: vanilla, raspberry and chocolate. Modern: plum and black cherry	$$	Spain's most famous region, currently reinventing itself to make fruit-driven rather than vanilla-driven wines
St-Emilion	Bordeaux	France	Merlot (plus Cabernet Franc & Cabernet Sauv)	Lush fruit with plums, redcurrant and blackberry, while the best show nuances of chocolate	$$-$$$	The 'Right Bank' appellation may be hip but generic Saint-Emilion ain't Le Pin at a low price!
Valpolicella	Veneto	Italy	Corvina et al	At its best, vibrant cherries, raspberries and spice. At its worst, watery and fruit-free	$-$$	The wishy-washy Valpol-Lite of the past is on the wane. Go for Classico and Ripasso examples

light   medium-bodied   full-bodied $-$$$ = bargain to bank-busting

Red wine flavor tree

Gamay
A grape with a smile on its face. Fresh and bulging with summer juices. The Beaujolais grape.

Tempranillo
Spain's top red grape: perfumed in Rioja, dark and dense in Ribera, concentrated in Toro – strawberries, plums, chocolate and smoke. Mmmmmm!

Cabernet Franc
Bordeaux's forgotten great. Violets, lead pencils, dust and perfume. Brilliant too in the Loire. For some reason overlooked, but capable of wines with great ageing potential and style.

Pinot Noir
Undoubtedly this is the world's trickiest red variety. Thin-skinned, site specific, fickle and temperamental it's at its best (and worst) in Burgundy where it makes some of the world's greatest, most gorgeously perfumed wines filled with the scent of strawberries, roses ...and a dollop of shit and mushrooms. (This is A Good Thing.)

Cabernet Sauvignon
The world's favourite red grape, Cabernet bestrides the globe's vineyards like some red colossus. The fact that it's at the core of the greatest clarets has meant that every winemaker has wanted to put his or her spin on its cassis, curranty, cigar-box aromas. Some – California, Australia – are succeeding (especially when they blend in Merlot, Cabernet Franc or even Shiraz to cut down Cab's naturally high tannins) but the cheap examples that pile up on the shelves are simply tedious Ribena lookalikes.

Corvina
The main grape behind Valpolicella. Can be light and industrial, but the best have a gorgeous, perfumed, cherry-like concentration.

Sangiovese
Chianti's own variety, Sangiovese blends well with Cabernet and is filled with the aroma of fresh cherries sitting in the Tuscan sun. Bizarrely, few outside Italy have bothered working with it.

Merlot
Currently the hottest red variety in the world, rich, plummy Merlot has long been the main variety in Saint-Emilion and Pomerol, No 2 in the Médoc and is now ultra-fashionable in California and Chile where it makes wines which are softer and more immediate than Cabernet.

Barbera
Grown across Italy (but best in the northeast) and bursting with plums, cherries and a fresh bite on the finish. Barbera's a good-time gal who just wants to be loved.

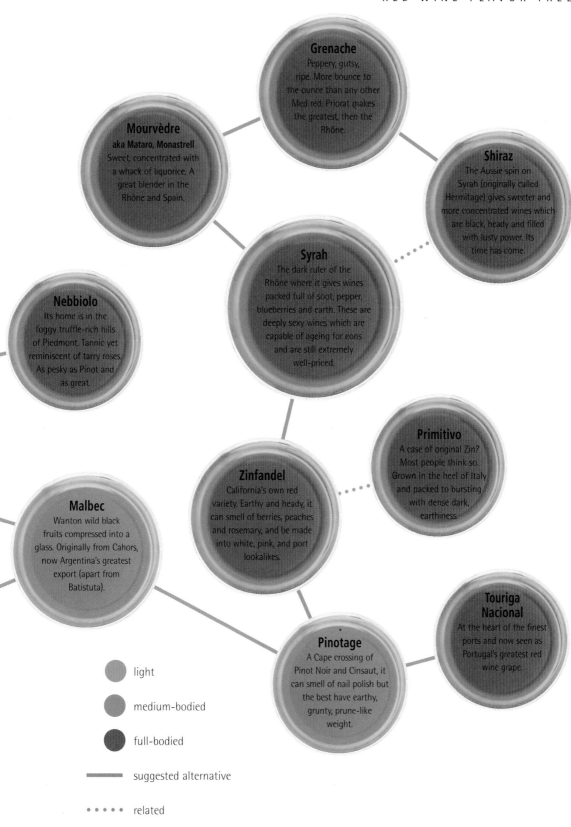

Grenache
Peppery, gutsy, ripe. More bounce to the ounce than any other Med red. Priorat makes the greatest, then the Rhône.

Mourvèdre
aka Mataro, Monastrell
Sweet, concentrated with a whack of liquorice. A great blender in the Rhône and Spain.

Shiraz
The Aussie spin on Syrah (originally called Hermitage) gives sweeter and more concentrated wines which are black, heady and filled with lusty power. Its time has come.

Syrah
The dark ruler of the Rhône where it gives wines packed full of soot, pepper, blueberries and earth. These are deeply sexy wines which are capable of ageing for eons and are still extremely well-priced.

Nebbiolo
Its home is in the foggy truffle-rich hills of Piedmont. Tannic yet reminiscent of tarry roses. As pesky as Pinot and as great.

Primitivo
A case of original Zin? Most people think so. Grown in the heel of Italy and packed to bursting with dense dark, earthiness.

Zinfandel
California's own red variety. Earthy and heady, it can smell of berries, peaches and rosemary, and be made into white, pink, and port lookalikes.

Malbec
Wanton wild black fruits compressed into a glass. Originally from Cahors, now Argentina's greatest export (apart from Batistuta).

Touriga Nacional
At the heart of the finest ports and now seen as Portugal's greatest red wine grape.

Pinotage
A Cape crossing of Pinot Noir and Cinsaut, it can smell of nail polish but the best have earthy, grunty, prune-like weight.

light

medium-bodied

full-bodied

—— suggested alternative

• • • • • related

Sparkling wine

Sparkling wines are the most difficult drinks of all to taste properly – after all, we'd rather swig them back in a carefree, careless fashion. **Bubbly** is a celebration drink, and it hardly suits such a frivolous, fun wine to get all serious about it. But precisely because it is brought out on important occasions, try to taste sparkling wine and **Champagne** before the big event. Anyone planning a wedding party, say, is strongly advised to buy some fizz and sit down and taste it while **sober**, to see if it's really worth the **cash**.

Bubble, bubble, toil and trouble

Short, fat, or long and thin? Although tall, narrow flutes are by far the best kit for drinking sparkling wine, when you're sitting down for a serious pre-party assessment, choose plain wine glasses which are all the better to swirl the fizz around for sniffing and tasting...

Chill out, man...

Actually, don't chill the bottle as hard as you would do for the event itself, as it might dumb down many of the wine's important flavor characteristics. Around an hour in the fridge is fine.

Watch out for low-flying corks...

Open the bottle carefully – remember the cork is under tremendous pressure, so point the top away from anyone when you ease it out (unless it's someone you dislike). Aim to make a soft 'pish' noise, not an explosion. The correct sound is known in the wine trade as 'a duchess' fart! Trickle a small amount down the inside edge and slowly into the bowl of the glass – easy does it, as sparkling wine has a tendency to spurt everywhere, as Michael Schumacher will attest.

Let's get fizzical

Once the glass is one-third full, give it a swirl and take a sniff. Sparkling wine should smell really appetizing, with a relatively light, elegant, fresh aroma. Some bubblies smell richer, fruitier, or creamier than others, but they should not over-power, like a blockbuster New World Chardonnay. Expensive sparklers should show some complex aromatics – yeasty depths, biscuits, light toast, cream, yogurt, as well as a myriad fruits from lemons to raspberries, depending on the grape varieties used (the more of the red grapes there are, the more raspberries you'll get – yup, you can use red grapes to make white fizz, as we'll explain).

Bubblicious!

If you're confident enough to avoid swallowing when you swish the wine around your mouth, get to grips with the flavor by taking a generous sip. Poor sparkling wines and Champagnes taste one-dimensional, often sharply acidic and lean. Great ones have a seductive, sensual and subtle combination of fruit, yeast, cream and fresh tanginess, all rolled into one multi-layered mouthful.

They're amazing. Then think about how long the flavor lingers on your palate, just as you would with any other wine; and how does it finish, fruity, crisp or dry?

How do I cater for old ladies?

Two other things to remember... The sweetness/dryness factor is very important here. Unless you're entertaining a bunch of toothless old hags who always demand extra sugar, you won't want to serve a sweet sparkler as an *apéritif*. And if you're serving fizz with dessert, you clearly want to avoid rasping, bone-dry bubblies. So think about that.

And, of course, you should always remember to consider the bubbles. No, bubbles are not all the same. Some sparklers are disappointingly flat. Others have enormous, coarse bubbles, as though a hippo has farted in the fermentation tank. The best sparklers (best because they are tantalizingly, delightfully crisp) have lots and lots of tiny beads of gas – a delicately fine mousse that continuously bursts all over the tongue and remains lively and luxurious right until the very last drop.

Champagne

Is it a bird? Is it a plane?

No! It's a Champagne cork, sailing through the sky, marking yet another celebration. It seems that nothing but fizz will do on certain occasions – frankly, you can leave the fine claret and top white burgundy at home. It's bubbly that we use to share life's happiest moments. That's partly because the pop of a cork heralds an event more joyfully than the creak of a cork-screw. And partly because the 'sparkle' sends the alcohol to your head more quickly than any other (bubbles mean the wine has more surface area for rapid absorption). Then there's the crisp, fresh character of dry sparkling wine – one of the world's most lip-smacking, whistle-clean aperitifs. And, of course, the kudos, inextricably linked to the scary price: we feel entitled to have an utterly fantastic time after spending a day's pay on a bottle of deluxe Champagne.

What's so good about Champagne?

Nothing measures up to the best mature vintage Champagne: Krug, Bollinger, Moët's Dom Pérignon, Roederer's Cristal, Pol Roger's Sir Winston Churchill, Veuve Clicquot's La Grande Dame. The chalky soil of the region (sparkling wine can only be called Champagne if it comes from one small region of northeast France), plus its cool climate, and the expertise of Champenoise winemakers, all play an important part. How can a wine be so fresh, elegant and subtle, and yet at the same time powerful, complex, rich and lingering? Champagne's exquisite mix of finely beaded bubbles and crisp acidity, plus notes of chocolate, biscuit and yeast, sometimes pulls off a difficult trick wonderfully well.

Tell me more...

Champagne can be made from three grapes: Chardonnay, Pinot Noir and Pinot Meunier. Pinot Noir gives structure, body and red-berry character, Chardonnay gives elegance, freshness and floral or yellow-fruit notes, and Pinot Meunier (the under-dog, not used in posher blends) is cheaper, and it can add fragrance.

Brut means dry; Extra-Dry means dry, but not as dry as Brut (confusingly), and Demi-Sec means medium-sweet. A prestige or deluxe cuvée is a house's top blend (eg Cristal is Roederer's prestige *cuvée*), and terms like *réserve spéciale* signify nothing except marketing speak.

Vintages vary a lot, so pick a good one. 1988, 1989 and 1990 were all superb.

CELLAR, GLASS & PLATE

Storing: Drink up light non-vintage Champagnes and cheaper fizzes quickly after purchase. They won't improve with time. Rich New World styles last a bit longer. Vintage wines are built to age: ten years is a great time to crack 'em open, but with more maturity they'll gain layers of toffee, honey and biscuit. Top non-vintage lasts a couple of years.

Serving: Chill all sparkling wine.

Matching with food: A classic *apéritif*, but it goes well with light canapés, fish and seafood (oysters!) served plainly or in cream sauces. Richer styles even stand up to white meat – try chicken.

The message in the bottle...

So bottle-fermented is better, right?

Giving the sparkle to sparkling wines – and Champagne – is a bit of a difficult trick. We're not talking about pumping carbon dioxide through a tank of white wine here. The *méthode traditionnelle* (which used to be called the *méthode Champenoise*) is an extremely meticulous process. It's not only used for Champagne – crémant, cava and many New World premium sparklers are all made in the same manner. The traditional method (look out for the words on the label) is supposed to create more complex, yeastily rich wine, by leaving the liquid to rest on its yeast sediment after second fermentation in bottle. And, fair enough, it does seem to be responsible for the most elegant, satisfying sparklers.

How does it work then?

A simple, tart white wine is produced from high acid grapes. It's bottled and sealed, along with a little sugar and yeast solution, which eventually kicks off a second fermentation, with the yeast this time producing carbon dioxide instead of alcohol. The carbon dioxide produced is trapped in the bottle (here come the bubbles!) and the yeast sediment, or lees, falls to the bottom of the liquid. The wine is aged for months on the lees, which gives it extra depth of flavor, perhaps yeasty, biscuity, even chocolatey nuances. The bottle is then held in an upside-down position, and the plug of sediment in the neck is frozen and popped out under the gas pressure when the cap is removed. A little sugar solution is added to top up the bottle, fill out the tart flavor, and control the sweetness/dryness level. Then the bottle is sealed with the distinctive cork and wire cage. Bingo!

Fizzio-therapy: other sparklers

Australia

The Australians love a glass of fizz and they don't think you have to wait for a special occasion to enjoy it. Inexpensive, home-produced Aussie bubbly can be fun, fruity stuff. But you'll have to spend more to get a fully-fledged, bottle-fermented fizz. Premium Australian sparkling wine is made with fruit sourced from the few cool-climate areas, most importantly Tasmania, the Adelaide Hills and Victoria's Yarra Valley, where Moët & Chandon's Antipodean winery is based. Top Aussie fizz is made from Chardonnay and Pinot Noir, and the best of it is surprisingly subtle and elegant, with toasty depths and a glint of ripe fruit. There are some surprises from Shiraz too – for more on this, see page 78.

England

English fizz used to be a joke, and with good reason, as most of it tasted like stewed cider. Now some truly impressive, Champagne-like, bottle-fermented sparklers are starting to emerge. It all makes perfect sense, of course. With its distinctly cold climate (and it's not so far from the Champagne region , after all), England can create exactly the sort of tart, acidic base wine that's needed. Tally ho!

France

We deal with Champagne, the real McCoy, on page 72, but is there a sparkle of decent fizz outside that small nook of northeast France? If you dismiss the morass of very cheap and cheerless sparklers, and look towards traditional bottle-fermented styles, then yes. The easiest route towards good-value, good-quality stuff is to look for the word 'crémant' on a label. This term, coined in the 1980s, indicates a bottle-fermented, lees-aged wine made under strict regulations in particular regions of France – Burgundy, the Loire, Alsace, Bordeaux and so on. Specific grape varieties are designated in each region – so Crémant de Bourgogne is made with Chardonnay and Pinot

It all makes perfect sense... With its distinctly cold climate, England can create exactly the sort of tart, acidic base that's needed for fizz. Tally ho!

Noir grapes, and tastes quite creamy and rich, while Crémant d'Alsace is often made from Pinot Blanc or Riesling and is more snappy and crisp. They're all well worth trying out, especially if you've got a batch of birthdays to celebrate...

New Zealand

Because of its long, cool, ripening season, as well as a culture of boutique wineries and designer cuvées, New Zealand is ideally suited to producing top-notch bubbly. The most exciting region for this style is Marlborough, where the sparklers taste as pure, fruit-driven and crisp

Where would we be without cava? Poorer, for a start, since cava is the undisputed bargain of the bottle-fermented wine world...

as those famous Sauvignon Blancs. Big-name wineries such as Cloudy Bay (supported by Veuve Clicquot), Hunters and Montana (with support from Deutz) all make serious fizz and sell it at fair prices. Good stuff.

South Africa

There's room for much more sparkling wine to be made in the Cape. A handful of wineries, notably in the Robertson and Franschhoek regions, have shown that South African bottle-fermented wine can take on the competition, but few have followed suit, and it's too hot in many areas to make acidic base wine. But, there's plenty of potential here, so if Australia can do it...

Spain

Where would we be without cava? Poorer, for a start, since cava is the undisputed bargain of the bottle-fermented wine world. Although it's made in the same manner as Champagne, the grapes used, Macabeo, Xarel-lo and Parellada, are decidedly Spanish. The wines are made and aged in huge cellars underneath the town of San Sadurní de Noya, in the Penedès region of eastern Spain. The result isn't especially complex or flavor-packed, but most cava is reliably fresh, sprightly, faintly appley fizz with an earthy hint. At around half the price of the cheapest Champagne, it's great stuff for sparkling cocktails as well as big parties.

USA

The cosmopolitan Californians do like famous-name fizz, so they've set about creating their own. The most successful top cuvées come from estates and vineyards based in (surprise, surprise) the cooler coastal regions. Expect high standards and even higher price tags, although some of the Champagne house spin-offs – like Mumm Cuvée Napa and Roederer Estate – provide very good value for the money.

But is it worth it?

Why does it cost so much?

If we were paid a dollar each time we were asked this question, we'd be able to afford... oh, nearly a whole bottle of Krug. It's that darned expensive. Champagne costs a lot because it's made in a labor-intensive and time-consuming way (see page 73); because you can only make a limited amount in that corner of France each year; and because competitive Champagne houses like to spend a lot on advertising and PR.

Fussy about fizz, moi?

Even Champagne can be lean and raw, with a sharp acidity – a dental and digestive nightmare. If it's too young, then bottle-age might soften it up and produce those creamy depths we all love, but then again, it might just remain enamel-rotting stuff. So there's the problem with fizz: some of it is sublime, some of it is a rip-off.

Shell out or sell out?

So, however light-headed you get on the stuff, it's important to make sensible decisions about such a pricey liquid. Don't shell out on extra-posh young vintage Champagne – it takes at least eight years to fully develop. Non-vintage (NV) is released ready to drink, so buy that if you can't find mature vintage. Our advice is to splash out on mature vintage champs only on special occasions when you'll savor it properly (say, a wedding anniversary), and go for NV when you want champagne style but can be less choosy (say, posh dinner apéritif). For events with more people (weddings, Christmas), go for a top New World fizz; its fruitier, easy-drinking character will go down well. French crémant and premium fizz from outside France are a good bet too. And, if you're on a budget, it has to be fresh, dry, appley Spanish cava, so stock up on that for parties and general piss-ups. The very cheapest European fizz is often nasty, and a rotten way to part with your cash. Lastly, give sparkling rosé or sparkling red a chance. Pink is more romantic, and red is more fun!

Fizz: other methods

How do the others get their gas?

The best sparkling wines are made by the traditional method, but how do the other bottles of fizz get their sparkle? Short of pouring a bottle of bubble bath into a tank of white wine and taking a straw to it, every which way you can imagine. Man has invented lots of methods to get carbon dioxide to flow in crisp streams of gas through wine.

In general, the standard of bubblies made by these other diverse methods is not as high as those made by the Champagne method, but there's the odd exception. Particularly when the second fermentation is done via the 'transfer method', which ranks as the second-best way to make fizz...

Transfer to where?

This mirrors the traditional method up until the moment of removing the lees. Let's face it, collecting, freezing, then disgorging the dead yeast from each individual bottle, and filling them up again with a little sugar solution is fantastically fiddly, and involves a ridiculous number of man-hours. Much easier to empty all

the bottles into a big tank, filter off the sediment all in one go, add the sugar solution to the lot, and rebottle the liquid. So the transfer method is cheaper than the traditional method, but nonetheless, it generally makes admirable fizz. The wine is still bottle-fermented and it picks up a good dollop of yeasty character from ageing on its lees.

Quick, dodge that tank!

Then there's the tank, or bulk method (otherwise known as the Charmat method, after its inventor) in which the wine is not bottle-fermented at all. The deed is done in large pressure tanks to which yeast and sugar are added. It's a cheap and cheerful way to make wine, which results in cheap and (if you're lucky) cheerful fizz, including Italy's Asti Spumante. But it does lack the complex yeast character of bottle-fermented sparkling.

The continuous method is another approach, and a weird one at that. The wine is passed through a series of tanks, acquiring its fizziness as it goes. When it enters the first tank, it has the sugar and yeast solution added to it. As it passes through the second and third tanks, the yeast sediment is removed.

Sparklers made in this way (mainly in Germany and Portugal) show some yeasty influence, but little finesse.

They really use bicycle pumps?

Deep down, you always suspected that sparkling wine was made by someone in a huge factory with a giant carbonation kit, and, here's where you learn you were right. The very cheapest sparklers are made by pumping carbon dioxide into wine. The result is crude, the bubbles extremely big and bouncing, and the complexity zero. The Melinda Messenger of the sparkling wine world.

And then there's the easy way

Finally, the ancient *rurale* or *ancestrale* method and the *dioise* method, in which wine is bottled while it's still undergoing the first fermentation – this continues in bottle, trapping carbon dioxide in the liquid. Wines tend to be sweeter and frothier than usual. They pop up (geddit?) around the southern French towns of Gaillac, Limoux and Die.

Pretty, pink and fizzy

Pink fizz? Don't be soppy...
Pink sparkling wine is not as fashionable as it used to be – except on Valentine's Day, when even the biggest, hairiest linebacker is happy to buy a bottle for his loved one. Aaahh! Although it's still seen as the epitome of romance, the rest of the year pink fizz tends to be ignored, which means people are missing out on delicious flavors.

Red sparklers are a quirky Australian speciality...try red sparklers with the Christmas turkey and stuffing for a laugh – they suit the food and the festive spirit.

Revive the rosé
We'd like to start a rosé revival – not just for still table wines, but for sparklers too. See, it's not just the image and the color of sparkling rosé that makes it stand out from the ocean of ordinary white fizz.

Vive la différence!
It smells and tastes different too. It's got a more pronounced aroma and flavor of red-berry fruit – strawberry, cherry, redcurrant, and above all raspberry. Great pink fizz, often made by blending a little red wine with white before the second fermentation, tastes like raspberry yogurt – ripe, creamy and fresh. Its color can range from very pale 'onion skin' to the orangey-red hue of a lurid sunset.

Does it work with food?
Try a dry sparkling rosé with lightly spicy oriental dishes as well as with shellfish. Fresh fruit needs a sweetish style.

And sparkling reds...?
Red bubblies are a quirky Australian speciality. Purple-colored, frothy and pleasantly peppery, even a little sweet, they are usually made from Shiraz grapes, although Cabernet Sauvignon and Grenache are occasionally pressed into service. Try them with the Christmas turkey and stuffing for a laugh – they suit the food and, somehow, the festive spirit. A few lighter sparkling reds are also made from Pinot Noir in California, and you may just come across a tasty frothy Italian red in the form of traditional Lambrusco (which is much higher quality than much of the stuff on supermarket shelves) and sparkling recioto, in the Emilia-Romagna and Veneto regions of Italy. Expect to see a surge in the popularity of red fizz.

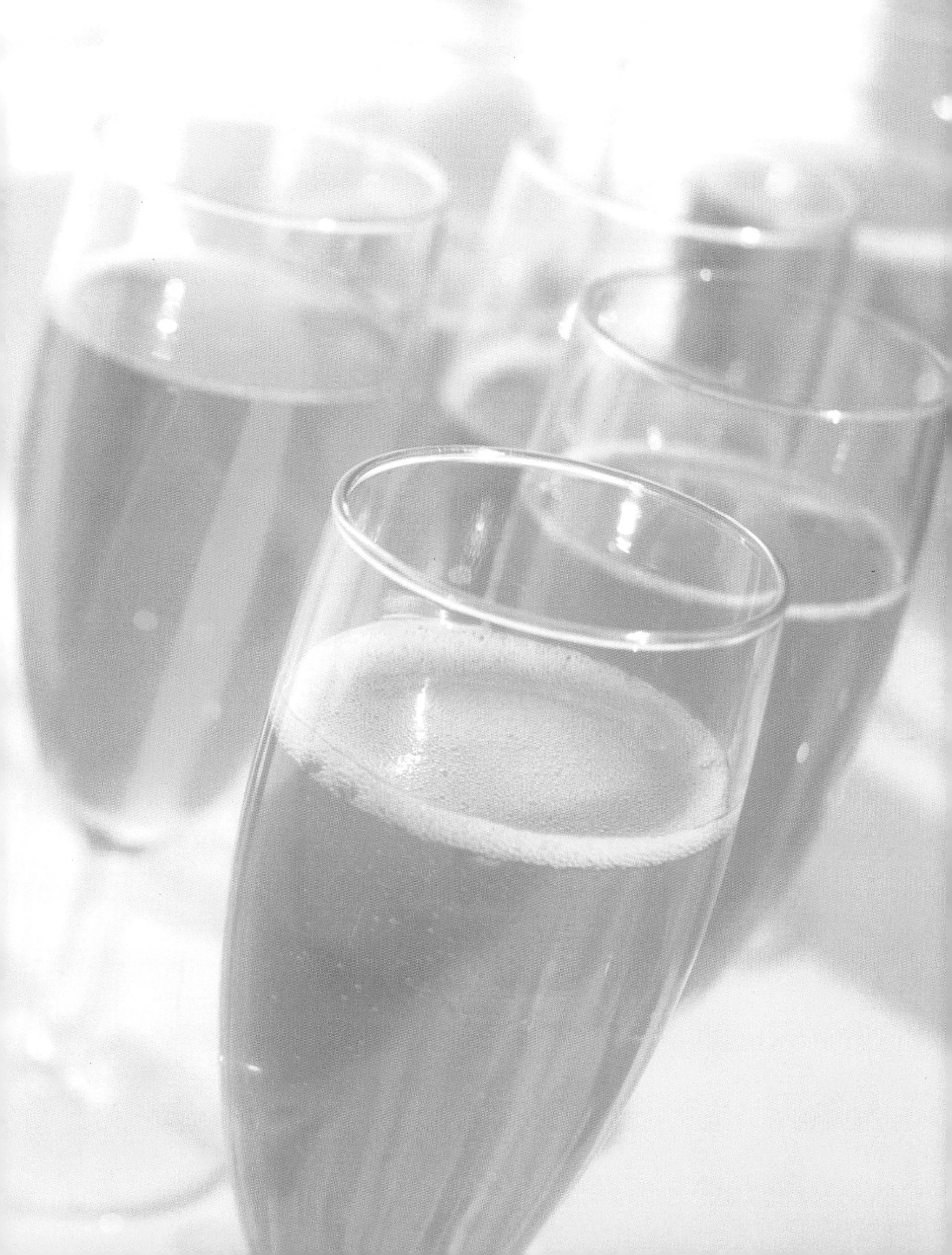

Sparkling wine styles

NAME	REGION	COUNTRY	GRAPE	TASTE	PRICE	ANYTHING ELSE?
Asti Spumante	Piedmont	Italy	Moscato Bianco	Quality varies, but hope for fresh, aromatic, sweetish fizz with the flavor of green grapes	$–$$	Try the superior, but less well-known Moscato d'Asti – creamier, better made and more tasty
Blanc de Blancs	Premium fizz areas	France and New World	Any white ones	More elegant, fresh and creamy than other fizz. Flavors of peach, apple, pineapple	$$–$$$	In Champagne, this means your fizz is made entirely with Chardonnay grapes
Blanc de Noirs	Premium sparkling areas	France and New World	The juice of any black ones	Fruity, forward, relatively aromatic and powerful. Flavors of raspberry, strawberry, cherry	$$–$$$	In Champagne, Pinot Noir & Pinot Meunier are the grapes used
Blanquette de Limoux	Southern France	France	Mauzac, Chardonnay and Chenin Blanc	Fresh, sharp, appley, sometimes creamy, sometimes faintly grassy and cidery	$$	Try local speciality Blanquette Méthode Ancestrale for a laugh. It's sweetish, cloudy and cider-ish
Cava	Penedès	Spain	Macabeo, Parellada and Xarel-lo	Fairly neutral, crisp. Faint note of fresh apple peel and, oddly, warm earth	$–$$	Chardonnay is now used in some blends to create creamier, fuller fizz
Champagne	Champagne	France	Chardonnay, Pinot Noir, Pinot Meunier	From the sublime to the rip-off. Elegant and fresh or full of creamy, mellow richness	$$–$$$	Drink non-vintage soon after purchase; vintage Champers will last much longer
Clairette de Die	Drôme, Rhône Valley	France	Clairette and Muscat	Lightly sparkling, dry or medium, refreshingly grapey	$–$$	The Clairette grape is no great shakes – bottles labelled 'Tradition' contain more Muscat
Crémant	Alsace, Loire, Burgundy, Bordeaux, Limoux	France	Various	Style varies from region to region, but crémants should be good quality, with some yeast influence	$$	These are the top French wines from regions other than Champagne. Often a bargain buy
Méthode Cap Classique	Western Cape	South Africa	Various	Fruity, fresh, often notably dry with good crisp acidity and plenty of citrus zest	$$	Several promising, top quality sparklers are now emerging from South Africa
Sekt	Various	Germany and Austria	Riesling, Pinot Blanc and Welschriesling	Beware nasty sulphurous cheapies, but Sekt can be elegant, racy, clean and fresh	$–$$	Try Sekt in situ while visiting Austria or Germany. It doesn't travel well

light   medium-bodied $–$$$ = bargain to bank-busting

Sparkling flavor tree

Méthode traditionnelle

Crémant
A newish breed of French wine – premium sparklers made outside Champagne but produced in the same meticulous way. Grapes may or may not be the same. Crémant de Bourgogne can be very Champagne-like; crémants de Loire and Alsace are fresh and crisp. Give 'em a go.

Spain
Spain's classic sparkler, cava, is made by the traditional method, and made from local grape varieties in the eastern Penedès region. Mostly dry, fresh, vaguely appley – and great value for money. The best fizz for sparkling punches and cocktails.

New Zealand
For pure, fruit flavors, crisp fizz and fresh acidity, it's hard to beat the New World sparklers now being produced by the traditional method in Marlborough on the South Island.

England
Cool climate = acidic grapes = perfect material for sparkling wine. The best traditional method English bubblies are surprisingly good.

South Africa
Méthode Cap Classique is the Cape's answer to Champagne. A few impressive fizzes, but why aren't there more?

Australia
Typical Aussie fizz is cheap tank method stuff, tho' some fine traditional method wines come from cooler areas like the Yarra Valley (Moët's Oz home). Price tag will help you decide which is which.

Champagne
Not a generic word for fizz but exclusively reserved for those from one corner of northeast France. The ultimate *méthode traditionnelle* sparkler? Can be a rip-off (especially the cheapest bottles), but top cuvées can be incredibly refined and rewarding – all your lovely lady ever dreamed of (even if they cost a week's salary).

California
The West Coast makes some very cool, sophisticated sparkling cuvées, from grapes grown away from the hotter spots. Impressive stuff – although many have scary price tags.

Australia
Don't miss the chance to try fun red (usually Shiraz) Aussie sparklers, and put some color into your bubbly.

Other methods

Méthode Ancestrale
aka Méthode Rurale
Sparkling wine produced simply by bottling young wine, which has not finished fermenting. Result? Sweetish fizz, often frothy rather than fully sparkling.

Transfer Method
Close to the Champagne method in that 2nd fermentation occurs in the bottle, but the contents are then transferred to tanks to remove the sediment before rebottling. Saves a few pennies; results are not quite Champagne standard.

Carbonation
Remember Soda Stream? This is wine with CO_2 pumped into it – using a tank, not a bottle. Makes crude, hyper-bubbly, very cheap fizz.

light

medium-bodied

red

suggested alternative

related

Méthode Dioise
Similar to above, but base wines fermented in tank very slowly and bottled to continue fermentation until lowish alcohol levels are reached, then disgorged, filtered and rebottled.

Continuous
Uses a series of pressure tanks through which the base wine plus extra sugar and yeast passes as the second fermentation takes place. Sediment is gradually deposited as it goes through this journey. Used for pretty basic fizz.

Charmat
aka Tank Method
aka Cuve Close
Popular and fast method of making cheap fizz in bulk. Sugar and yeast added to base wine in big pressure tanks, fermentation stopped by cooling the wine, which is then clarified and bottled. Bingo.

Fortified and sweet wines

Be prepared to enter a **forgotten** world which operates under a different set of rules. Get ready to learn to **love** wines that smell of nuts, mushrooms, dried fruits, barley sugar and rotting apricots. Start to appreciate new flavors that redefine intensity, **gaze** into a world ruled by wines that can apparently last for ever and **discover** why the letter 'M' has put a hex on some of the greatest, most ancient fortified wines on the planet. Put aside prejudice. Plunge into the weirdest wines of all.

Look, linger, lick and love

So 'fortified' wine, that's a mixture of wine and brandy isn't it? What a great idea for a guaranteed hangover! Actually there's good reason to add brandy to wine. In the days before rapid transportation, wine had to be able to stand up to long journeys, often in high temperatures, thereby running the risk of being spoiled en route. Since wines with high alcohol levels are stable, producers began adding brandy to those which were going to travel long distances.

Pump up the volume

Fortifieds fall into two camps. You can either pump up a wine's strength by adding the spirit before the wine has fermented dry, which gives you a sweet end product; or fully ferment the wine, then add the alcohol, to give you a dry fortified. Port is made the first way, most sherry the second.

Pretty old-fashioned though?

Sadly true. Fortified wines are deeply unfashionable, seen as the preserve of crusty colonels, country vicars and maiden aunts – and no-one could ever accuse any of those as being arbiters of good taste. That said, at least you stand a chance of being offered a glass of port or sherry every so often: if you want to find the Madeira, Málaga or Marsala you have to look at the back of the kitchen cupboard beside that bottle of sticky Malaysian soy sauce that was only ever used once. Hip they ain't.

Dried up and useless?

Actually, that reminds us, there's another branch which is half-way between fortified and sweet wine which is made by drying grapes either on mats or trays to concentrate their sugars and increase the alcohol. It's an Italian speciality, known as *passito* and it's used for a whole number of different grapes. Recioto and amarone are the most commonly seen wines – the Italian equivalent of port with no added spirit. Passito the port you could say.

You could, I wouldn't...

But why bother with fortified wines these days? Because the best examples give a glimpse into a different, slower world miles away from today's culture of instant gratification and upfront, fruity wines that can be drunk by the pint without making an impact. Fortifieds are intense, strong wines built to be enjoyed in small sips, over long periods, when they can lubricate the imagination and fuel conversation.

Sherry

Not for me, thanks

It's a sad fact that the only people who love sherry are those who either live in Andalucia, or write about drink. It's entirely up to you if you want to believe us, but you should give sherry a try for the sake of the hospitable Andalucians, people who seem to need only one hour of sleep a day and have an insatiable appetite for life. It's sherry which fuels their non-stop partying.

OK, convince me...

Sherry is the most frustrating, confusing and seductive drink of all.

The production is plain weird, it comes in a mass of styles with confusing names, yet when you open your mind you discover a wine which is about essences of flavor, of new levels of freshness, intensity and pleasure. A fino is the driest wine you'll ever try, a Pedro Ximénez (PX) the sweetest. All wine is here.

Uno Palomino blanco

In between Seville and Cádiz is a bleached out, parched, landscape of hazy chalk hills, brilliant blue skies and relentless summer heat. You'll also find one grape variety dominates – Palomino. All sherry (except that used for sweetening) is made from this grape. It all starts normally enough. The grapes are lightly pressed, their juice is fermented giving a light, boring white wine. Now the weirdness begins. The producer decides which of this wine he wants to turn into fino and which into oloroso. Olorosos are fortified to over 18% and put into casks in a solera (we'll explain that in a second). Finos are fortified to around 15%, also put in casks, and we then wait for the "flor" show.

Great sherry contains every flavor you could ever want in a wine. Finos taste of salted almonds, amontillados of hazelnut, olorosos have notes of walnut...

Huh?

The surface of the young fino begins to be covered by a thick layer of white yeast, known as 'flor', cutting the wine off from air and keeping it light and fresh. This swaddling blanket is kept alive by moving the wine regularly through the solera system.

Huh? (again)

Imagine a room of full barrels six high and many accross. Each horizontal row contains wine of the same average age, with the oldest at the bottom. If you want a case of sherry you take the required amount from the bottom row. Then you top up the missing amount with (younger) wine from the row above and so on. This allows the wine to be blended, for it to have consistent style, and it keeps the flor alive. Olorosos are moved less frequently, so are darker and nuttier, without the fino's freshness.

What about amontillado then?

Let the flor die and the wine will start to oxidise, darken and take on a dry, nutty character. That's an Amontillado. Now it gets confusing. All sherries are dry, but commercial amontillado and olorosos have been sweetened with concentrated grape must, or treacle-sweet wine made from dried PX grapes.

Pale cream is a blend of fino, amontillado, grape must and charcoal (to take the color out). Nice, eh? Creams are olorosos with PX added.

True love starts here...

Great sherry contains every flavor you could ever want in a wine. Finos taste of salted almonds, amontillados of hazelnut, olorosos have notes of walnut. Finos are bone dry, totally fresh, and in the case of manzanilla, salty and made to be drunk ice-cold. The greatest amontillados and olorosos are sipping wines that have been reduced to their intense essence. Fall in love with sherry and nothing else can quite match it.

Port

Know the bishop of Norwich?

No? Neither do we. Though if someone asks you that question when you have a decanter of port in front of you, it is meant as a subtle hint to pass it to them, which only underlines the fact that when it comes to a sense of the surreal, the English upper classes are in a league all their own. It's not surprising that this bizarre question should be associated with port. No other drink is so crusty (in every sense) and full of arcane rituals known only to gout-ridden, Tory-voting gentlemen slumped in leather armchairs at their clubs, muttering about the decline of the British Empire. A shame, since port is a silky, satisfying mouthful of headily perfumed, sweet and spicy red fruits. It's time for the masses to reclaim it.

Right on comrades! Tell me more

Imagine a wildly beautiful gorge lined with steep terraces hewn into the slate that's home to dark colored, thick-skinned, flavor-packed grapes. That's the Douro Valley in northern Portugal and those grapes: Touriga Nacional, Touriga Francesa, Tinta Barocca and Tinta Roriz (aka Tempranillo), are the backbone of port. Harvesting is quite a feat – making it takes quite a few feet.

There's a joke in there somewhere

Sorry. It's just that traditionally, once the grapes were picked, they were (some still are) trodden under foot in large cement tanks called *lagares*, as the human foot is actually the gentlest way of extracting tannin and color. There's even one winery with an automatic foot! You need to get as much color and flavor out as quickly as possible because the fermenting yeast are stopped with brandy when the wine is still a sweet little baby. It's then either matured in wood or in bottle.

Accounting for all those styles?

You got it. Vintage, which is only made in the top years from a blend of wines from the top single estates (*quintas*), is aged in barrel for 18 months and then transferred to bottles where it continues to mature. It isn't ready to drink until it's at least 10 years old. No wine is so enormous. It fills the mouth with flavors of pepper, spice and wild berry fruits, liquorice and a firm structure. If you're not able to shell out $40 or more for a bottle, try a single quinta vintage instead. These ports come from the best quintas, and usually make wines which constitute the heart of the finest vintages. They tend to be lighter in style than true

CELLAR, GLASS & PLATE

Storing & Serving: Tawnies should be lightly chilled, while vintage, single quinta and traditional LBV need to be aged on their side, stood up the day before serving, then decanted to remove the thick crust (spread it on toast the morning after). Tawnies can be enjoyed for a couple of weeks after opening, LBV for a week, vintage only for a day or so.

Matching with food: Nibble almonds with tawny (or try it with soup or creamy pudding). Vintage etc is best at the end of a meal, on its own or with strong cheeses and nuts.

vintage and mature more quickly – but they cost less. Be careful though. There are some excellent small single estate producers who quite correctly use the term quinta as part of their name. If you want a vintage single quinta, ensure the label says 'vintage'. These port styles need decanting and are for special occasions. The best port for everyday consumption is late-bottled vintage (aka LBV). It's like a scaled-down vintage, with that exotic signature perfume, spice and plummy, sloe-berry, instantly-appealing richness. Unless it says 'traditional' on the label, LBVs don't have to be decanted – which is another great advantage.

What about tawny?

It's the one where the port has spent a long time ageing in oak casks. Make sure it's at least 10 years old, or from a single vintage (aka Colheita). Tawnies nuzzle up to the best rich oloroso and amontillado sherries as they show touches of nut and a fine, intense acidity. They're the most versatile port style of all: equally at home as an aperitif or as an after-dinner drink.

What about that tart Ruby?

'Ruby' is young, often harsh and best ignored. Oh, there's also white port which, though good, is best drunk in situ and not on a rainy day in Barnsley.

I'll buy a bottle next Christmas...

No! Port, like a puppy, isn't just for Christmas but for any day of any week. Look at it this way, if it is such a magnificent end to a meal at one time of the year, doesn't that show it can do the same whenever you have a fine feast?

So why do you pass port to the left?

Haven't a clue. It could be an ancient Celtic custom to keep away evil spirits; it could be because it's easier to pour something that's by your right hand... You decide. But for goodness sake, keep passing it. You don't want to make the acquaintance of that bishop do you?

More fortified wines

There's something 'bout an M

There must be some curse on this letter. Four of the greatest fortified styles: Málaga, Madeira, Marsala and Montilla, are all close to extinction, while liqueur Muscats and *vins doux naturels* made from the same variety, ain't exactly well known.

Andalucia to the arse-end of Sicily

Montilla, from near Cordoba, is a 'sherry-style' wine made from Pedro Ximénez, at its best when full-on, molasses-sweet and venerable. The third great Andalucian fortified wine, Málaga, has been hideously bastardised so that the wines seem to be made from charred raisins sweetened with boiled must, although one superb dried-grape wine has recently appeared but, sadly, production is tiny. The situation is little better on Sicily, home of Marsala, a wine that's only ever mentioned when someone says 'zabaglione', and that's not often. Look for labels with Vergine on them, or the wonderfully named Terre Arse.

Dog stranglers and black moles

Then there's Madeira. This rock in the Atlantic produces wines with such astounding power and levels of acidity that they can last for millennia. In the days of Empire it was discovered that Madeira tasted better after it had been slooshing about in the stuffy, hot holds of ships on their way to India. Ever since, it has been heated, either in tanks called *estufas* or in casks in the rafters above the estufas. Standard Madeira is made from Tinta Negra Mole, but look for varietal wines: Sercial (related to a variety called 'dog strangler') is searingly acidic; Verdelho is all walnuts and apples; Bual richer, and Malmsey raisined. One of the world's greatest wines.

Tin sheds and marmalade

The last 'M' is for Muscat. Australia's magnificent fortified speciality, liqueur Muscat, hails from Rutherglen, a place of high temperatures, baked earth and tin-roofed sheds with cobwebby barrels nestling beneath. It's like liquid Olde English marmalade. In France, the same variety makes lighter *vins doux naturels* (VDN) where the ferment is stopped when the wine has plenty of sugar left. Muscat de Beaumes-de-Venise famous, but also try Muscats from Rivesaltes, Lunel, Mireval, or Frontignan. The greatest VDNs.

CELLAR, GLASS & PLATE

Storing: Nothing here the equivalent of vintage Port, though Banyuls will certainly improve with cellaring. Madeira, because it has already been 'cooked', can be enjoyed for weeks once opened, if not months.

Serving: Liqueur Muscats, Madeira and Málaga: serve at room temperature. Marsala, Muscat and Banyuls can be lightly chilled.

Matching with food: Christmas pudding and chocolate for Rutherglen Muscat and Banyuls; hard cheeses, nuts and a period of contemplation for the other 'M's.

Fortified flavor tree

Oloroso/Cream
Great olorosos have an intense flavor of walnut and raisin. Cream sherries are olorosos with a dollop of sweet PX, while pale creams are sweetened finos.

Vintage
The pinnacle of the port producers' portfolio, vintage is only produced in the very best years. It matures in bottle and normally isn't worth drinking before it's at least a decade old.

Colheita
A little-known vintage tawny style. More intense and nuttier than vintage but with equal depth.

Amontillado
True amontillado is an aged fino and is therefore dry. It's also deeper and nuttier.

LBV
A vintage style but able to be drunk when young. Start here.

Sherry
One of the greatest and most misunderstood wines in the world. Sherry ain't a drink for maiden aunts and neurotic vicars but a wine to be savored and loved.

Port
From some of the world's most spectacular vineyards, port is a wonderfully versatile winer. Like a puppy it's not just for Christmas.

Fino
The driest sherry — and that means bone dry. Thirst quenching and compulsively moreish, no home should be without a half bottle in its fridge.

Tawny
Classically, a port that's been aged in cask. Try it chilled.

Madeira
Piercingly clean, Madeira is like a cross between port's perfumed richness and sherry's intensity. Not just with cake.

Ruby
It's meant to be young and vibrant, but rarely is.

Manzanilla
From the coastal town of Sanlúcar de Barrameda: lighter and drier than fino, with a salty tang that makes you immediately want another glass (or bottle).

non-Jerez 'sherries'
Some dreadful drinks have passed themselves off as 'sherry', the worst being British. Australia and South Africa, however, make some cracking alternatives.

Málaga
Spain's forgotten fortified. Dark, liqouricey and burnt, it is barely clinging on to life. Save it please!

non-Portuguese Ports
The greatest come from South Africa and (even better) Australia. Superb wines in their own right.

Montilla
Not poor man's sherry but a slightly richer Andalucian style. The PXs are magnificent.

Vermouth
A French and Italian speciality made by fortifying white (or red) wine and then macerating herbs (traditionally wormwood) in the mixture. Noilly Prat is vital for dry Martini cocktails.

Marsala
Traditionally off dry and from Sicily and now more often seen in the kitchen than on the table. A brave rearguard action is being fought.

Liqueur Muscat
An Australian speciality from Rutherglen, and, tasting like liquid Christmas pudding, this is one of the world's great wines.

Banyuls
Take the Beaumes-de-Venise recipe and apply it to red grapes.

Beaumes-de-Venise
Rhône speciality: honey-ripe with a little boost of spirit.

○ dry

○ medium-dry

○ medium-rich

○ rich

○ violet

○ ruby

○ tawny

—— suggested alternative

····· related

Botrytised and other sweet wines

Attack of the vampire spores

It's like something out of a Stephen King novel. The autumnal mists rise off the river during the night, inveigling themselves into the rows of vines, wreathing their shadowy tendrils round the golden globes of the grapes and then, like some evil vampiric incubus, leave miniscule spores on the skin of the fruit. Rot starts to take hold, sucking away the water in the grape, gnawing away at its skin. A covering of fine ash begins to appear, then the fruit darkens and begins to turn to mush, draped with cobwebs of grey, hanging on the vine like a witch's shrivelled dugs. You get the idea. For centuries any grape grower seeing that hellish scene happen would shout 'Botrytis!', pick the grapes and hope for the best – or throw them away and spend a miserable winter cursing his luck...

A load of rot

The world of *Botrytis cinerea rot* is a weird one. The grapes may not be a pretty sight, but the rot mutates the grape, concentrating its sugar levels, preserving its acidity, increasing its glycerol and giving the end wine a strange aroma, flavor and feel.

There are notes of apricot, barley sugar, wax, and mushroom. The wines smell sweet yet decayed. This isn't any old rot, matey, this is NOBLE rot.

Sweet surrender

Making botrytised wines ain't simple. The method's like this. One: find a vineyard near a body of water (as in Bordeaux's Sauternes or Barsac, or near the River Loire, or Germany's Rhine or Mosel, Hungary's Tokaji-Hegyalya) or Austria's Neusiedlersee. Two: ensure that in the autumn there are morning mists which burn off during the day. Three: grow grapes with thin skins and high natural acidity (try Sémillon, Sauvignon Blanc, Chenin, Riesling, Furmint). Four: employ pickers who are (a) not bothered by bees and wasps and (b) willing to go through the vineyard day after day picking off individual rot-affected berries. Noble rot doesn't hit every bunch (or even every grape) at the same time. Five: be prepared to wait. Making sweet wine is a slow process. High sugar levels mean yeasts take ages to work their way through the thick, gloopy juice. Eventually they just give up, leaving a wine with what geeks call high

CELLAR, GLASS & PLATE

Storing:

Great sweet wines will last forever and benefit from as much cellaring as you can bear to give them. Lighter styles will age for just a year or two.

Serving:

Serve them chilled but not frozen...

Matching with food:

Sweet wines don't go with sweet foods (generally speaking). But very light, tangy sweeties go with fruit desserts and botrytised Sémillon is fab with chocolate puds. Try richer botrytised wines with blue cheese and pâtés instead.

Rottin' all over the world

residual sugar (ie, it's bloody sweet) but still with buckets of mouth-freshening, life-giving acidity.

Where in the world?

The greatest (or most famous) botrytis-affected wines are the barley-sugar, apricoty, lime-zest examples from Sauternes and Barsac, but you should also check out the ageless, unctuous honey, wax and quince wines made from Chenin in the Loire Valley – areas like Coteaux du Layon, Quarts de Chaume, Bonnezeaux and Vouvray. Allow botrytis to hit Riesling in Germany and you have magnificent sweet yet steely wines made as *Auslese,*

Beerenauslese (BA) and *Trockenbeerenauslese* (TBA). In our minds BA and TBA from Austria are even greater. Producers on the shores of the Neusiedlersee lake working with a huge range of varieties make botrytis-affected wines of amazing concentration. In the premier league is Tokaji which comes from around the town of Mád in northeast Hungary. These are legendary wines where the paste of rot-affected grapes is added by the basket – the baskets are called *puttonyos* – to fermented base wine. The end result can, allegedly, revive the dead. The more *puttonyos* on the label, the sweeter the wine. Rich, teasingly dry,

sweet yet austere, like *tarte tatin* with a nutty pastry crust.

Sugar spun sisters

Not every sweet wine is made from grapes affected by botrytis for the simple reason that not every region has the right conditions (the correct, 'noble', form of botrytis is very particular after all). There are, however, plenty of other ways to make sweet wine. The ones which give the best results revolve around ways of dehydrating the grapes. The most commonly seen term is 'late harvest' which means the grapes have been allowed to shrivel on the vine. It's a technique that suits hot,

The grapes are either tanned outdoors on mats, like tourists on the beach, or, in the cooler north, taken indoors and dried there like washing on a rainy day...

dry areas where rot-filled mists are unlikely to appear. The wines tend to be less complex with purer flavors.

Eiswein a go-go

Eiswein uses the most masochistic winemaking techniques of all. If you like getting up at 6am on a freezing winter's morning to go and pick grapes then you're a penguin short of an ice flow, but Germans, Austrians, Swiss and Canadians think it's fun. Most of the frozen water remains inside the grape, so the result is superbly pure, clean and intensely sweet wines and very high price tags.

Pass the passito

The last technique is the oldest of all: drying the grapes. Originally a Greek idea, this method, called *passito*, is used across Italy and produces complex, strangely perfumed wines. The grapes are either tanned outdoors on mats, like tourists on the beach, or, in the cooler north, taken indoors and dried there like washing on a rainy day. The sweetest come from the southern islands of Pantelleria and Lipari, and are made from Zibibbo (Muscat); while the most astoundingly multi-faceted are the Vin Santos from Tuscany, which can be sweet, dry, even sherried. Even reds get in on the act. In the Valpolicella region, Corvina grapes (with partners Rondinella and Molinara) are dried in trays and turned into either sweet Recioto or drier Amarone. These are magnificent alternatives to port: all black cherry concentrate layered over rich, muscular structure. These aren't pudding wines, they're coda wines or, as the Italians rightly call them, *vini da meditazione*.

Sweet flavor tree

Eiswein
Masochistic speciality which involves picking frozen grapes under cover of darkness. German... but also Canadian.

Sweet Germans
Made from Riesling that's been left to hang in the late autumn sun. Honey-coated apples, rich but not cloying.

Moscato
Italy's most versatile grape. The lightest are frothy, grapey and perfumed. A wine to make you grin insanely.

Barsac
Every bit as good as Sauternes. Chill and sip.

Saint-Croix du Mont
Clean, easy-drinking, straightforward sweetie.

Jurançcon
From the far southwest of France. Honeyed and lush.

Chenin
The Loire's contribution. Sometimes with noble rot added, sometimes without. Subtle richness.

Sauternes
Heady and hedonistic: apples, apricots, rot (the best, most 'Noble' kind), barley-sugar and acidity. The world's greatest sweet. wine, which battles Cabernet Sauvignon and Merlot for vineyard space down in Bordeaux, France. Anyone for foie gras and blue cheese?

Monbazillac
Not as complex as Sauternes but with richness. Best before a meal.

Muscat
A wine that smells of grapes! and of jasmine and fresh fruit. Dreamy, soft but never too heavy.

Tokaji
Legendary, complex Hungarian rot-filled speciality. Can allegedly cure ailing royalty.

Late Harvest
The New World version of VT (see right).

Vendage Tardive
Alsace's greatest grapes left on the vine to build up their sugar levels. Concentrated, powerful.

Muscat (Zibibbo)
Take Moscato, dry it in the sun, make wine, discover jasmine, marmalade and white mushrooms in the glass. Zibibbo!

Vin Santo
Tuscany's holy wine. Dried grapes fermented in sealed casks in the attic. Lifts you to another dimension.

Recioto
Italy's best-known dried grape red (sweet = Recioto, dry = Amarone). Sloe berries, chocolate, cherries. Port? Who needs it!

Dried Grapes (non-Italian)
Search out Greece's Vin Santo and root out New World examples from Victoria and California.

Dried Grapes (Italian)
Italy's oldest style and made across the country. Wines of wild, heady concentration.

- light and sweet
- sweet and fresh
- sweet and sticky
- rich and sticky

——— suggested alternative

· · · · · related

Fortified wine styles

NAME	REGION	COUNTRY	GRAPE	TASTE	PRICE	ANYTHING ELSE?
Amontillado sherry	Jerez	Spain	Palomino	Intense, roast almond/hazelnut aromas and flavors. Dry	$$	True amontillado is an aged fino. Commercial styles are actually medium-sweet olorosos
Cream sherry	Jerez	Spain	Palomino	Thick, raisined, velvety	$–$$	Old-fashioned, moribund style. Try PX or oloroso dulce instead
Fino sherry	Jerez	Spain	Palomino	Bone dry: chalky, bready, green olive, Parmesan, lemon pith	$–$$	The greatest aperitif in the world. Have it ice-cold and drink quickly
LBV Port	Douro	Portugal	Touriga Nacional and other natives	Wild berries, incense, herbs. Exotic and ripe	$$	Port for those who can't afford vintage every night. Look for the label 'traditional' (ie, unfiltered)
Liqueur Muscat	Rutherglen	Australia	Brown Muscat	Raisins and Olde English marmalade	$$	Still one of the great bargains of the wine world
Malmsey	Madeira	Madeira	Malvasia	Richly sweet, concentrated, with tingling acidity	$$	The most widely-seen Madeira style (also try ultra-dry Sercial, softer Bual and medium Verdelho)
Manzanilla	Sanlúcar de Barrameda	Spain	Palomino	Light, bone dry, lemon-fresh with a salty finish	$$	You can tell this comes from the seaside by its salt-tinged finish. Perfect with prawns
Montilla	Andalucia	Spain	Pedro-Ximénez	All the way from full nutty pale dry, to rich molasses-sweet PX	$–$$	Underrated style, at its world-class best as ultra-sweet PX
Oloroso sherry	Jerez	Spain	Palomino	Full-bodied and concentrated: walnuts, spice, prunes and raisins	$–$$	True oloroso is dry, but most is sweetened
Tawny port	Douro	Portugal	Touriga Nacional and others	Cheap: light, soft, bland. Aged and vintage (colheita): intense, nutty, perfumed	$–$$$	Tawny should be aged, but cheap versions are just lighter rubies. Look for aged or colheita
Vermouth	Savoie	South France North Italy	Various	French tend to be white, herbal and delicate; Italian red, either bitter or sweet	$–$$	You can't make a Martini without Noilly Prat
Vintage port	Douro	Portugal	Touriga Nacional and others	Perfumed: sloes, wild berries, herbs, liquorice, spice	$$$	Made in the best vintages, ready to drink after 10 years. Single estate (quinta) are excellent value

dry   medium-dry   medium-rich   rich $–$$$ = bargain to bank-busting

Sweet wine styles

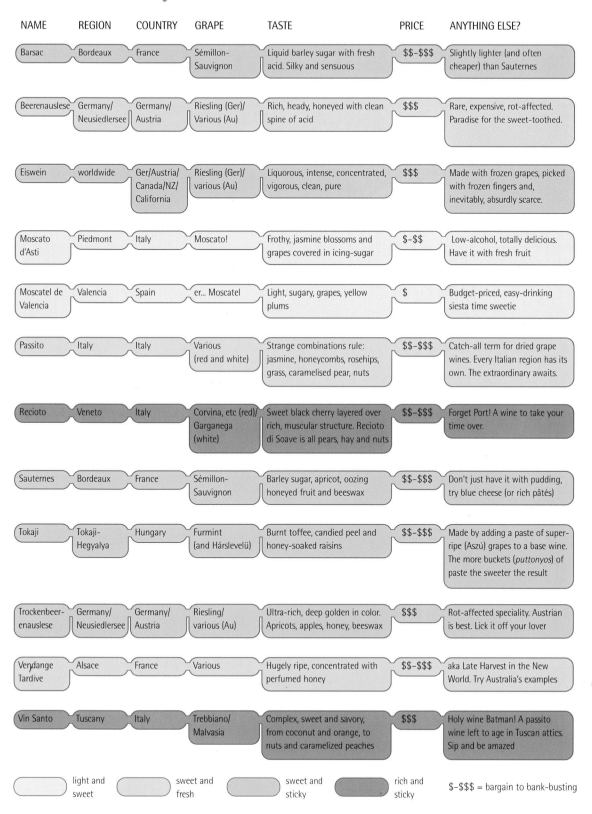

NAME	REGION	COUNTRY	GRAPE	TASTE	PRICE	ANYTHING ELSE?
Barsac	Bordeaux	France	Sémillon-Sauvignon	Liquid barley sugar with fresh acid. Silky and sensuous	$$–$$$	Slightly lighter (and often cheaper) than Sauternes
Beerenauslese	Germany/Neusiedlersee	Germany/Austria	Riesling (Ger)/Various (Au)	Rich, heady, honeyed with clean spine of acid	$$$	Rare, expensive, rot-affected. Paradise for the sweet-toothed.
Eiswein	worldwide	Ger/Austria/Canada/NZ/California	Riesling (Ger)/various (Au)	Liquorous, intense, concentrated, vigorous, clean, pure	$$$	Made with frozen grapes, picked with frozen fingers and, inevitably, absurdly scarce.
Moscato d'Asti	Piedmont	Italy	Moscato!	Frothy, jasmine blossoms and grapes covered in icing-sugar	$–$$	Low-alcohol, totally delicious. Have it with fresh fruit
Moscatel de Valencia	Valencia	Spain	er... Moscatel	Light, sugary, grapes, yellow plums	$	Budget-priced, easy-drinking siesta time sweetie
Passito	Italy	Italy	Various (red and white)	Strange combinations rule: jasmine, honeycombs, rosehips, grass, caramelised pear, nuts	$$–$$$	Catch-all term for dried grape wines. Every Italian region has its own. The extraordinary awaits.
Recioto	Veneto	Italy	Corvina, etc (red)/Garganega (white)	Sweet black cherry layered over rich, muscular structure. Recioto di Soave is all pears, hay and nuts	$$–$$$	Forget Port! A wine to take your time over.
Sauternes	Bordeaux	France	Sémillon-Sauvignon	Barley sugar, apricot, oozing honeyed fruit and beeswax	$$–$$$	Don't just have it with pudding, try blue cheese (or rich pâtés)
Tokaji	Tokaji-Hegyalya	Hungary	Furmint (and Hárslevelü)	Burnt toffee, candied peel and honey-soaked raisins	$$–$$$	Made by adding a paste of super-ripe (Aszú) grapes to a base wine. The more buckets (*puttonyos*) of paste the sweeter the result
Trockenbeerenauslese	Germany/Neusiedlersee	Germany/Austria	Riesling/various (Au)	Ultra-rich, deep golden in color. Apricots, apples, honey, beeswax	$$$	Rot-affected speciality. Austrian is best. Lick it off your lover
Vendange Tardive	Alsace	France	Various	Hugely ripe, concentrated with perfumed honey	$$–$$$	aka Late Harvest in the New World. Try Australia's examples
Vin Santo	Tuscany	Italy	Trebbiano/Malvasia	Complex, sweet and savory, from coconut and orange, to nuts and caramelized peaches	$$$	Holy wine Batman! A passito wine left to age in Tuscan attics. Sip and be amazed

light and sweet sweet and fresh sweet and sticky rich and sticky $–$$$ = bargain to bank-busting

Beer

Beer is, sadly, seen as a commodity these days. Massive multinational brewers churn out identical gassy brews which aren't worth a second look. But get below that bland surface and a new world opens up, every bit as **complex** and **rewarding** as wine. Beer too has its traditions, craftsmanship and **myriad** wonderful flavors. The good news is that as the big **brewers** get ever bigger, so small independents are pushing the boundaries out once more, creating new – and rediscovering old – styles. **Let's** go find them!

Pour, pause, gaze, quaff

It's different to wine tasting isn't it?

Actually it isn't. Just as tasting wine involves using all of your senses, so appreciating great beer requires your ears, eyes, nose and mouth. Ears? Just think of that pop as the cap comes off a bottle, the hiss, gurgle and splash as the bartender starts pouring. Then there's waiting for the turbid foam to settle in a glass of stout, the pause as you look at the ruby red pint of bitter topped with a full, creamy white head. If that isn't enough to get your mouth watering then you have no soul.

But does it have the legs?

A beer should look good. Ales and lagers should be clear and bright; stouts thick, dark and creamy. Even beers which are meant to be cloudy, such as wheat and lambic, should be bright, enticing and not flat and dull. As for the depth on the head of a pint of bitter, we'll leave that up to you.

Keep cool, man

Think of red and dark ales as being like red wines, lagers like whites. Pale ales and bitters are best at a coolish temperature; lagers, wheat beers and golden ales should be lightly chilled. The British are beginning to catch the same disease as the Australians, who probably caught the infection from the Americans, and are serving beers at temperatures close to freezing. OK, it masks the fact that there's bugger-all flavor in most standard brews in the first place, but ice-cold stout is plain bizarre.

Get your nose working

Few of us take any time sniffing our pint glass, but the idea that this sort of behavior is restricted to strange men with beards and anoraks is like saying the only people who like wine have cut-glass accents and wear pinstripe suits...

Steady-on old chap...!

If you don't give your beer a sniff then how can you pick out the sweet, toasty, malty nose of a great Scottish ale? The appley tartness of an IPA? The cloves and bananas lurking in a great wheat beer? This is something you want to DRINK.

Swallow don't spit

Even if the beer has seemingly not touched the sides of your gullet you'll have noticed the flavors. The sweetness at the front of the mouth, the drying fresh bitterness of the (all important) hops on the finish as it slips down. Each style has its own character: the sweet and sour attack of a great Belgian ale, the hoppy surge of an IPA, the roasty richness of a creamy stout, the fresh perfumed bite of a great Pilsner. Once converted you'll find there are as many variations in beer as in wine.

Raise your glasses...

An all-important vehicle to beer-drinking pleasure. You may start getting obsessive, taking your holidays in Belgium or touring the hop fields of England, insisting on the right glass for the job. You don't have to take things that far, but the following is a helpful guide. Ales are best in straight pint glasses, and lagers in tall, thin, straight-sided ones, but try barley wine in a red wine glass, and fruit beer in a Champagne flute. Each Belgian brew has its own unique glass – not just for marketing kidology but to enhance some aspect of the brew... the head of Duvel or a wheat beer, the aroma of a trappist ale.

Is a hat really necessary?

As for jamming a wedge of lime into the neck of a bottle, it's a bloody good idea, given the beers it's done to... at least it gives them a bit of flavor.

Lager

Lager? It's just yellow beer isn't it?

Wrong! The first ever lagers were dark beers, like ales. The term 'to lager' means to rest – originally, German brewers would take their beers into mountain caves in the summer to avoid them going off. Even today, all lagers will undergo a similar period of cold maturation which may be as short as a few weeks or up to a few months. Thanks to refrigeration, caves are no longer needed, though no doubt there's a pioneering American brewer in the Rockies or Alaska who is attempting to recreate this ur-lager style.

When the beers were stuck in their icy caves, the yeasts sank to the bottom of the barrel and, over time, brewers realised that the bottom-fermenting yeasts worked in a significantly different way to the top-fermenters used in ale production. These bottom feeders mutated in order to be able to live and continue working at temperatures which would kill their top-fermenting brothers. While the latter stopped working and died as soon as the temperature began falling, the bottom fermenters would keep on working away, slowly eating more of the sugars in the beer. The result of this was a drier drink – which may have lost some of the rich, fruity notes that signify a great ale but replaced them with a clean, fresh and (most significantly) dry aroma and flavor. These were clean, palate-cleansing beers that were miles away from the rich, often heavy ales of the time.

Hop for happiness

It's not that there are no hops, just that since this beer is a lighter and more delicately flavored brew, so more fragrant and less astringent hops such as Saaz or Hallertrau tend to be used. It all depends on the style – you'll find some lagers with a fair whack of hoppiness to them.

But lager is lager, surely?

You'll certainly think so if you've only ever drunk the bland, fizzy alco-pop that's foisted on us by the industrialised brewers, but the Czechs and the Germans know that there are as many lager styles as there are ale. It's just that as lager has overtaken beer to become the world's favorite

---

CELLAR, GLASS & PLATE

Storing: Hmmm, in a fridge!

Serving: How to serve lager? Get real! Shove a six pack in the fridge, rip off the tab and chug back. Not too far off the mark, but try and buy bottles (because they are small, the beer stays cold to the bottom of the glass and doesn't end up tasting like a hamster). And go for Czech or German lagers, still the most flavorsome and the most classy!

Matching with food: Over to you!

Lager flavor tree

Danish
Very, very mild, often pretty neutral. Tuborg is average, Ceres better. The best is Carlsberg Elefant (which is a Bock, not a Pilsner).

Belgian Lager
Decent, lightly hoppy lagers in a delicate Pilsner style. Stella is good, but Maes and Cristal Alken are the best.

Dutch Lager
Pilsner by name, but in a lighter style. Grolsch is the best, but try Christoffel for a hoppier variant. Drink ice-cold with a jenever.

American Lager
The big brewers make sweet, light Zen lagers (the taste of nothingness). Stick to the specialities from the microbrewers.

Diat Pils
First brewed for diabetics (not slimmers). Holsten is the specialist.

Pilsner
Never has a name been so misused. Pilsner was first brewed in Bohemia (now in the Czech Rep) in 1842, in what is now the Pilsner Urquell brewery. The Bohemian style is a little malty, but has a cracking flowery-hoppy aroma and a crisp, dry finish. Traditional Pilsners include Urquell, Gambrinus, Staropramen, Velke Popovice and Kruseovice. The Germans, if anything, increased the emphasis on hops, but each region puts its own spin on things. Pilsners from the north are the hoppiest of all, Baden ones are lighter and dry, while Pilsners from Bavaria are big, malty bruisers. There's a host to choose from, but Radeberger, Bitburger, Jever, Spaten, Warsteiner and Konig are among the best. Although the name Pilsner appears on hundreds of brews from around the world, most bear as much resemblance to the genuine article as Boyzone do to Led Zeppelin.

Australian Lager
For a country that loves its beer, Oz makes some dreadful, chemical-tasting brews. Sydney's Scharer and Melbourne's Matilda Bay are exceptions.

Helles
A classic, light-styled, utterly refreshing German speciality, particularly from around Munich. A summer lager to be drunk with gusto. Go for Augustiner, Löwenbrau and Hofbrau.

British Lager
First brewed in Scotland in 1875, but practise hasn't made perfect. Gassy, bland, strangely fruity, low in strength. Most 'foreign' lagers sold in the UK are brewed in the UK and fall into the same boring style.

Commercial Dark Lagers/Dunkel
A spicy, malty, dark brown brew first brewed in 1840 in Munich. The best German ones are: Spaten; Prinz Luitpold and Ayinger. If you like the style, also try U Fleku from the Czech Republic; Bayer from Norway or Xingu from Brazil. Dunkel is another style popular with American microbrewers.

Bock
The true-strong lager and an amber-colored malty, sweet, headily potent brew. Great with food. Look for Einbecker, EKU, Paulaner and Kulmbacher (all German); Aass (Norwegian); Samichlaus (Swiss) and a host of US microbrews.

Strong Lager/ Malt Liquor
Artificial, headache-inducing sugary concoctions. Our advice is to steer clear. If you want strong lager, drink a Bock.

Vienna Style
(Aka Marzenbier/Oktoberfest) Russet-hued lovelies, first brewed in Vienna. Soft and malty and now a Munich-brewed speciality: Spaten and Sedlmayer are the greatest, but red lagers pop up across the world – Dos Equis in Mexico; Aas Jule Ol in Norway and throughout the US microbrewery community.

Budweis
Another Bohemian beauty and a sweeter, less-hoppy variant on Pilsner. Budvar, Zamek and Samson are the ones to look for. Budweis is no relation to Budweiser.

Doppelbock
The strongest of strong lagers. Malty and dark, as sweet as pie and with a kick like a mule. Try Paulaner Salvator (or any other Munich brand ending with 'tor'). But treat with respect.

Dortmunder Export
A cousin to Pilsner and Helles, but less aromatic than the former and crisper than the latter. The beer that kept the German foundries rolling. There are few producers left, so get searching for DAB and DUB from Dortmund and Sapporo's Yebisu. Yet another style that US microbrewers have turned their enthusiastic attentions to, with some good results.

lightest

light yellow, drier and fragrant

gold, drier still

red/amber, malty

dark

 suggested alternative

style, so the subtleties between the different drinks have been forgotten. Take Pilsner. You probably think this signifies a piss-weak, bland and low-priced concoction with zero flavor and zero personality, instead of a richly flavored, fragrant brew that's brimful of character. This, the original golden lager, was a Czech creation, or, to be precise, a genuinely Bohemian beer from the town of Pilsen. It was such a success that everyone else decided to imitate it and, over time, the name became bastardized and used to give a spurious credibility to the mass of ersatz 'pilseners' you find today. We say, stick to the classic Pilsners from the Czech Republic and Germany! In fact, there are probably more styles of lager than you ever imagined. There are dark lagers, ruddy lagers, dry lagers; lagers which are off-dry, light, or strong and mentally brutal...

I like that wheat lager

Glad you do, but it's an ale not a lager.

Lager, lager everywhere

Australia

Australia takes lager into a dimension which says beer should be so cold it freezes your teeth and gives you a hangover before you've even finished your first pint. Stick to Cooper's Sparkling Ale or seek out the few microbrews.

Belgium

Belgium has tended to specialize in its vast offering of ales, lambics and fruit beers. There are some semi-decent Pilsner-styles.

Britain

British lagers are mostly international brand names brewed in the country under licence and are pitifully poor.

Czech Republic

The Czech Republic is home to the original Pilsner, aka Pilsner Urquell, one of the world's greatest beer styles that hits a superb balance between fragrant dry hops and soft maltiness. Head to Prague and start exploring its great bars to see what beer's all about.

Denmark

Science met with ancient knowledge in the Carlsberg laboratory in 1845, where the first strain of bottom-fermenting yeast (*Saccharomyces carlsbergensis*) was isolated, thereby allowing lager production to start its world domination. While most Danish beer is disappointingly light, stronger versions (usually labelled with exotic African animals) can be marvellous.

Germany

The tightest beer laws in the world, the most breweries and the widest range of lagered beers. Choose from bone-dry pilsners from Hamburg, or the lighter examples from the wine growing areas of the Rhine, strong, crunchy Dortmunder, or the mass of beers hailing from that Mecca of brewing, Bavaria. There you can find dark (*dunkel*) lagers, delicate malty Helles, the full-flavored Fest beers, up to the strong bock or even stronger doppelbock. If you want to find out what lager really tastes like, start here.

Holland

Dutch brewing is dominated by Heineken, but some good smaller brews exist. The lagers are on the softer, lighter side of the spectrum.

USA

Mass-produced American brews are fine examples of the dumbing down of lager. Flavorless, with virtually no alcohol, they are soda-pop beers for the non-discerning drinker. Thankfully there are microbrewers who are rediscovering real lager. Seek 'em out!

Beer flavor tree

Aussie Sparkling Ale
Australia's greatest beer. A second fermentation in the bottle gives complex flavors: tart, hoppy, malty. Beloved by winemakers.

Lambic
An ancient beer made from wild yeast. Crisp, sometimes sour, citric, fresh. Geuze is a blend of old and young and has a natural fizz to it.

Wheat Beer
This ain't lager either. Made from wheat and using ancient yeast strains (giving it clove-like aromas) the freshest (and most tart) is Berliner.

IPA
Much abused term. IPA was an export ale, so was strong and very highly hopped to help it to last the sea journey. A revival of real IPA is taking place, particularly in the US.

Bitter
The English style. The bitterness comes from the aromatic, tannic hops. The color can be gold, russet or mahogany; the bitterness can be intense or gentle, the alcohol low or high. The best include Timothy Taylor's Landlord, Young's Special, Adnams Extra, Smile's Best.

Fruit Beer
Usually a lambic beer refermented in cask with fruit (any fruit), though Belgian brown ale can also be used. A great aperitif.

Pale Ale
Reddish, complex, nutty ale whose home is in Burton (Bass, White Shield, Marston's). The best ales are coming from US microbrewers (Sierra Nevada): they're dry and refreshing with great bite.

Belgian Red Ale
Like IPA, the closest style to rye whiskey with a vicious whiplash of acidity. Utterly refreshing and individual. Rodenbach is the greatest.

Wheat Beer
The complex, refreshing Bavarian wheat beers smell of cloves, bananas, fruit and lemon (Erdinger, Schneider Prinz Luitpold). The Belgian style (Hoegaarden) has citrus peel and coriander added.

Mild
Gentle, lower in alcohol than bitter, darker and sweeter. A thirst-quencher for the proletariat. Highgate and Bank's are the finest.

Porter
A light, dark-colored London ale made with roasted malt – a southern mild. Enjoying a mini-revival among microbrewers in the UK and the States.

Wheat Beer
Dark wheat beer? You must be mad! Wonderful rich Christmas pudding aromas with a fresh finish.

Scottish Ale
Maltier (and less hoppy) than English ales, the rich, sweet Scottish ales operate under arcane terminology of 'shillings': 60/-mild, 70/-heavy, 80/-export and 90/-old ale, used to show the amount of tax levied on a barrel. Search out anything from Caledonian, Traquair, Belhaven 80/- and 90/-, Maclay's 60/-.

Stout
Originally a strong porter, now Ireland's greatest beer. Guinness is roasty, hoppy yet creamy on draught; Beamish is lighter and more like chocolate; Murphy's is in between.

Brown Ale
Best-known is Newcastle Brown Ale, an off-dry, malty brew beloved by Geordies and bikers. Elsewhere (Mann's, Sam Smith's) are sweeter.

Barley wine
The sweetest, richest most liquorous style. High in alcohol and gaining in favour in the States.

Sweet & Imperial Stout
Stout's version of IPA, strong roasted charred fruit. Still made in the Baltic (and by Courage and some Americans). A strange, (thick and sweet) offshoot: Mackeson, Tennent's Sweetheart.

Flemish Brown Ale
As intense as a palo cortado sherry, mixing tartness and dried fruit. The best is Liefmans. Also used as a base for fruit beers.

Trappist
Today, six monasteries make these strong bottle-conditioned brews. Chimay the best known and richest; Orval the driest. Abbey beers, like Leffe, are secular homages.

Bières de Garde
Northern French farmhouse speciality. Malty, slightly spicy and great with food. Jenlain and Ch'ti the best known.

○ lightest

○ light yellow, and fragrant

○ gold, drier still

● red/amber, malty

● stout

▬▬▬ suggested alternative

• • • • • related

Ales and stout

The only ale-ment you'll ever want

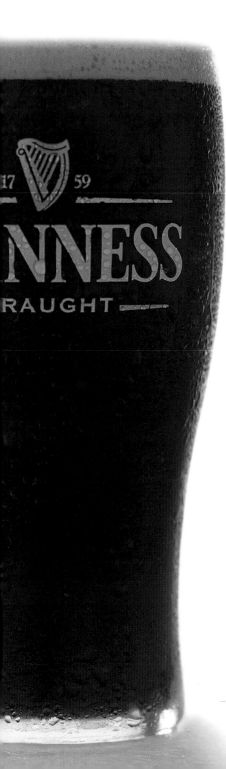

Ale? It's a brown beer isn't it?

Well, strictly speaking no. An ale is a beer that is made from top-fermenting yeasts, so it can come in a huge array of colors and flavors. What's remarkable is the way in which such simple ingredients – water, yeast, hops, malted barley – can be transformed into such a range of styles.

OK, how is it made?

Beer is a product of that magical grain, barley, which – when it has germinated – starts turning its starch into soluble sugars. By then drying the barley (kilning) you can create different types of malt. A light kilning is good for pale lagers, but malt for pale ales will be left a little longer. If you kiln the grains when they're still wet they'll start cooking and crystalizing, getting darker in color and producing more intense, nutty flavors. Leave them long enough and they start roasting (Guinness is made from roasted malt) and then, like potatoes left in the oven, they virtually carbonize – giving the chocolate malt used in porters. Brewers can then blend the different malts, just as a winemaker in Bordeaux uses different grapes.

Mash it up!

The malts are ground and hot water is poured on to give a sugary, sweet liquid, which is then brewed in a cooker with hops. These are incredible little flowers that not only help preserve a beer, but also give bitter, citric tartness and perfume. The earlier you add the hops to the brewing, the drier (more bitter) the beer will be. Then yeast is added.

BUYING ALE & STOUT

Ale: Buy by the bottle if you can, it's a great way to discover what treats the best of the smaller regional and independent brewers are producing. Look out for 'bottle conditioned' on the label; these have had a little dose of yeast added to give a sparkle.

Stout: We still believe that stout is best on draught, but if you want the bottled version, look for Guinness' strong and more bitter export styles, or take a bet on bitter/fruity Imperial Stout. Tennent's Sweetheart is worth finding if only for the label... well actually, only for the label!

The top-fermenting stuff...

You got it. Ales are made from yeasts that rise to the surface, so technically everything other than lager (including wheat beer, lambic and stout) is an ale. Because top-fermenting yeasts aren't as good at eating all the sugars and esters in the fermenting liquid, ales tend to be slightly sweeter than lagers, with more lifted aromas. After a week or so of fermenting, most of the yeast is skimmed off and the ale ferments ('conditions') a second time.

So what makes them different?

It might be the water, it's certainly the malt recipe, the amount of hops, when they are added, the strain of yeast and the conditioning. Brewers can play a vast number of tunes on a pretty simple recipe. Go to a decent pub in Britain or the States and the choice is overwhelming. It's impossible to keep tabs on how many microbreweries are operating these days, though lots seem to be run by well-meaning home brewers working from the same manual. Still, the time has never been better to get out and explore the world of ales.

But I'm a wine drinker

Don't say that in the presence of a winemaker. There's nothing they like better after a hard day tasting than a PCA (that's Palate Cleansing Ale by the way). The Australian wine industry has single-handedly kept Coopers sparkling ale in production. Once you learn to love flavor, you'll love DRINK.

Stout's a strange name in these PC days

While some Californians may want to call this classic brew 'big boned beer' the name, according to beer expert Michael Jackson (no, not that one), came about because stout was originally a stronger style of porter that was 'stouter' in flavor. It all happened when maltings were used to produce a more heavily toasted malt, which gave porter and stout not just their color but their distinctive dry, roasty-toasty flavor.

Fat porters? It's getting worse!

Now porter, beer historians claim, was a dark-colored style of English ale from the 18th century that had the characteristics of a number of beers in one glass. It was popular with porters in the London markets because it was lower in alcohol, and so, like the thirst-quenching milds that were the staple beer in the steel towns of the Midlands, not only did

In recent years there's been an attempt by the Welsh to claim stout as their invention... Right enough, they are trying to claim that Elvis was Welsh as well!

it slake the thirst but workers could drink large quantities of it, quite often using it to wash down vast quantities of oysters – the fast-food of the day. Strangely vile modern mutant beers like Caffreys – the color of an ale, the temperature of a lager and the head of a stout – are today's twist on the porter legend.

Isn't it Irish?
In recent years there's been an attempt by the Welsh to try and claim stout as their invention...Right enough, they are trying to claim that Elvis was Welsh as well! For the rest of us, stout is the Irish drink par excellence, and no country in the world produces such superb examples. It all started back in the 1770s, when Arthur Guinness started making the style**.** So popular was the beer that he switched his entire production to making the black gold 20 years later.

Is the best in Dublin?
Now there's a question. A lot of the quality of a good Guinness is down to how it is stored and served, though Dublin Guinness is made slightly differently to British. In many ways it's like drinking *rosado* in Spain: one sip of this dry, black, silkily bitter beer in a Dublin pub makes you instantly more loquacious. That said, there's a huge number of different versions of Guinness on the market. Forget the marketing scam of ice-cold draught and look for the bitter, bottle-conditioned version and the marvellous, strong 'foreign' Extra, both of which are astoundingly good with Cheddar cheese.

What of the pretenders?
Don't say that in Cork, where Murphy's makes a softer, less roasted stout and Beamish, the sweetest, most chocolatey version of all. There's minor revival in Yorkshire and Scotland where softer, nutty oatmeal stouts are reappearing. Tennent's and Mackeson still persevere with their milk stouts, though real beer lovers rightly swear by the potent dense, smoky, burnt sweetness of great Imperial stouts. Porters are seeing a minor revival among small, forward-thinking brewers in the UK and the States. Like oysters, they may never become the preferred drink of the masses, but their reappearance is to be welcomed.

Wheat beers

Wheatzuppp?

Wheat – or white – beers are enjoying a new wave of popularity. Great – these are some of the most refreshing and thirst-quenching beers we can think of. It would be a great shame if they disappeared into obscurity. In London, the rise of the *moules-frites* Belgo chain of restaurants has put Belgian wheat beer firmly back in the limelight, and across the 'pond' in the USA and Canada, 'wheat beers' are now being made.

Wheat beers are rarely made from wheat alone, but with a proportion of barley. One theory says that brewers always had trouble prising enough wheat off the bakers, whereas barley was more readily available. Others believe wheat is a more difficult brewing ingredient. Whatever the case, beers made partly with wheat are paler and tend to produce a very lightly colored foam during fermentation, hence the alternative name 'white beer'.

So all white on the night then?

They range more widely in style than you might think. The most obvious difference is between those wheat beers which derive their character from specific yeast strains (think German wheat beers) and those that get their distinctive flavor from the addition of spices and citrus peel (Belgian wheat beers). Some are cloudy and some are clear. Most are top-fermenting and designed to be drunk chilled, while they are young and ultra-fresh.

Like a virgin

Belgium

Perhaps because Belgium used to be part of the Netherlands when it was an important spice trading country, Belgian wheat beer is characterised by the addition of coriander seeds and curaçao orange peel. The most famous Belgian wheat beer is Hoegaarden, made in a lovely old brewery near Brussels since the 15th century. And lovely is the beer too – a cloudy, creamy-white, lightly frothy and slightly sweet, thirst-quenching draught with a fruity finish. This is typical of the Belgian style of wheat beer (aka *witbier* or *bière blanche*).

Germany

In southern Germany, wheat beer (or *Weizenbier*, or *Weisse*) has been made for at least a thousand years. It's fruity in style, with a hint of clove (which comes from the yeast used). It's often fermented a second time in bottle and unfiltered (like fine sparkling wine). This is known as *Hefe-weizen*. Filtered wheat beers are called *Kristall Weizen*; dark wheat beers (made with wheat and dark malt) are called *Dunkel Weizen*; strong beers are called *Weizenbock*. Berlin's '*Weisse*' is pale, sparkling and high in acidity – known for centuries as the 'Champagne of

the north'. Sometimes it is mixed with raspberry syrup, or a green herbal essence, or it is served in big bowl-like glasses as a summer *apéritif*. It undergoes a 'lactic fermentation' like many wines, to convert the appley malic acid into creamier lactic acid.

Others

A few breweries in Austria, France, Switzerland and Holland make wheat beer. In the States and Canada, micro-breweries imitate the German styles, often with impressive results. We've even found wheat beers from New Zealand and Australia.

Speciality beers

All beer's made the same way today

Not true. There's one branch of the family which hasn't changed since the earliest days of brewing. The Belgian producers of lambic beer located around the River Zenne are the most ultra-traditional in the world – and their beer is magnificent.

Tell me more...

Lambic brewers rely on wild yeasts to trigger the long, slow ferment. Basically, they put the brew (made from wheat and hops) in the attic, throw open their windows and wait for the yeasts to pitch in. Then the beer is put into ancient oak barrels, also with their own resident yeasts, and starts to ferment, sometimes for years. It's brewing that's never lost touch with its roots. Because of the nature of the production, it is also the only beer which has a season (or vintage): October to March. A true lambic is a young beer that's stunningly fresh and acidic, and not for the fainthearted. But you're more likely to come across gueuze – a blend of aged and young lambics which has had a second ferment in bottle and may also have been slightly sweetened, but is still complex, fresh and tart – between a dry white wine and a beer in flavor; it's the beer equivalent of Champagne and probably predates it!

But this one tastes of cherries!

Lambic beers (and brown ales) are often used as the base for yet another Belgian speciality, fruit beers. Any fruit can be used, but cherries (*kriek*) or raspberries (*frambozen*) are the most frequently seen. They're added to the fermenting casks and the beer ferments on top of them. They are bone dry, almost tart, yet full of soft, fruity flavors. Adding fruit, herbs or spices to beer is an old technique. Belgian wheat beers have added orange peel and coriander, but these days brewers are using all manner of fruits for fruit beers, though the brews made by just adding essences of some exotic berry or fruit taste artificial and false. The fashion is spreading from its Belgian roots. You find wonderful heather ale in Scotland, gooseberry beers from England, (we're not wholly convinced about these, to be honest). In the States, microbrewers have leapt on the idea of fruit beers with unabashed glee. Chilli, honey, ginger, marijuana, cranberry, all have been used, with differing degrees of success.

Cider

Cider with Susy & Dave

All cider is a lurid orange color, tastes artificial and sweet, and fizzes violently, right? Well, no, actually, but if you've drunk mass-produced cider in a bad English pub, you'd be forgiven for jumping to the wrong conclusion. How can one of the great English drinks have been brought so low? Nowadays it is associated with under-age drinking, headaches and 'snake-bites' – a gruesome but effective blend of cider and lager. But delectable cider does still exist. Find it in great country pubs around the UK, buy it in Normandy along with your calvados and cream, or get it straight from the farmhouse either side of the Channel. It isn't always fizzy, but either still or very faintly spritzy. It isn't always clear – cloudy scrumpy is acceptable, unlike cloudy wine. And it can be crisp and dry or mellow and sweeter, and range in color from very pale to autumn gold. But decent cider always conjures up harvest-time, with its wonderful, authentic scent and deeply refreshing flavor of ripe, juicy apples, something the bulk-produced fizzy stuff never does.

What's the difference then?

Mass-produced cider is made from apple concentrate, which can come from anywhere, and it's made all year round. Of course, it often contains additives. And it can be diluted, pasteurized and chaptalized (sweetened). Genuine farmhouse cider is made with local apples (usually a blend of different cider varieties – blending is an important part of the cidermaker's craft). With time-honoured simplicity, the apples are harvested, ripened, and pressed, and the juice is passed into vats to ferment naturally. After a few months, it is taken off its yeast sediment and put into barrel for another few months. Just like a fine wine, in fact.

Apples of your eye

Britain

Ignore the luminous orange stuff produced by the big boys and look for real cider – many supermarkets now stock premium bottled cider (or 'cyder') from small, family-run companies. Watch those alcohol levels – seven or eight percent is not unknown, and that's similar to a light German wine. The best ciders, in our view, come from Gloucestershire, Herefordshire and Worcestershire.

France

A wonderful tradition of cider making in Normandy continues to this day. Many Normandy ciders are pale, sweet, fine, and bubblier than English ones. Some of the best are bottle-fermented, like Champagne. The French take cider seriously and don't produce as much commercial gloop as the British do.

Spain

In the north of Spain, around the Asturias Mountains, an ocean of cider is produced for the thirsty domestic market (we've never seen it exported). It's light, pale and slightly sour stuff, which locals pour from a great height into small glasses to aerate it, often missing completely. Refreshing after a mountain hike, but no great shakes.

USA

A little cider is made in the USA, but much of it is non-alcoholic, bizarrely. Alcoholic stuff is called 'herd cider'.

Spirits

Spirits entertain the **senses** with a wide range of looks, **smells** and flavors – from clear, through golden, to mahogany in color; from odorless, through fruity, to fiery in **aroma** and taste. There is a spirit to suit everyone, whether your **tipple** is a marvellous malt or tasty tequila. And everyone has the ability to **taste** – you just follow a few rules and let your mind flow.

A short, sharp sniff & a sip

Strangely, even though people might be happy tasting wine, tasting spirits is seen as bizarre behavior. To most of us spirits taste of...well, spirits. But treating all whisky (or gin, or vodka) the same is like walking into a music store, grabbing a CD at random and buying it 'because it is music'.

So, how do you do it?

Everyone knows how to taste – you just follow a few rules and let your mind flow. You use all your senses, but the bulk of the work is done with the nose. Think of the glass of spirits as a jigsaw puzzle of aromas and flavors that you have to assemble in your mind. Every sniff or sip gives you a clue to where the spirit is from, how it has been made, if it has been aged, how old it is... oh, and whether it is any good.

When shall we three meet again?

It is always best to taste at least three spirits – three gins, three vodkas, three malt whiskies, or maybe one Irish, one bourbon and one malt. The rules differ slightly for each type, but you always start by giving the neat spirit a short, sharp sniff and noting the initial aromas. Then, if you are tasting Scotch, gin, brandy or cask-strength bourbon, add a little water – still mineral water, never tap water. (Vodka, tequila, rum and standard-strength bourbon lose their aroma if you dilute them.) Adding water makes the neat spirit go slightly hazy and a coiling mass of threads appear in the glass. These are ester chains, breaking up and releasing their complex aromas. How much water you add is also down to personal taste, but it's best to start with a little drop and add more if necessary. Don't just pour the water in – you're liable to drown the spirit.

Free the spirit

Scientists have so far discovered 300 flavor compounds in malt whisky, all of which can be detected by the nose. The key is to lock into the main aroma and then analyze it. It may be peaty (the barley has been dried over a peat fire – see page 110) but does it smell of iodine or tarry ropes, bonfires or sea-shells? Perhaps it smells of flowers, apples, cut grass or hay – these suggest a lighter dram. A gin will smell of juniper, but what else? Lavender, sage, citrus peel? These all show what kind of botanicals (see page 117) have been used.

Now make it personal

Embroider the aroma with your own memories. Whisky often smells of the 'outdoors' – a Highland moor, or a salt-lashed coastline. Smells, especially those from childhood, never leave your memory. Use them. The smell of your granny's chest of drawers won't mean anything to anyone else, but it will help lock that aroma in your mind.

Can I taste it now?

Roll it round the mouth to discover its texture: mouth-filling, oily, creamy, crisp? What's the dominant flavor: sweet, sour, tart, dry? Good quality spirit will be complex and balanced, not spirity and one-dimensional. Then swallow. Does the flavor disappear suddenly or does it last for ages?

There's no one correct answer...

But conversation is the best way to get everyone's senses working overtime, so taste with friends. Be warned, once you've got a nose for it, it's difficult to stop!

Whisky

1) sweet and estery — pear-drops? complex, full of finesse, flavors of bananas and cream sodas delicate whiff of peat.

2) light and fragrant — blossom, heather, honey, some spice. ... but finish is

3) fudge and toffee-like, some citru notes and definite hint of ginge little smoky? Full-bodied an immensely smooth

4) light colour and body green, herbal notes, slight gently sweet overall mou excellent aperitif whisk

Whisky

Malt whisky's made from barley?
Spot on. Distillers have always used their most common surplus crop. In Scotland and Ireland's case it happens to be barley. Malt whisky is made from malted barley (barley which has undergone a controlled germination to break down the tough cell walls), water and yeast. The malted barley is dried, maybe over a peat fire, then ground into flour, has hot water poured onto it, giving a sweet liquid called wort, then yeast is added to make a strong beer which is distilled twice in copper stills. In the second distillation the 'heart' – the clean, pure spirit – is separated from the heads and the tails, and this is then aged in used wooden barrels. Simple!

The flavor's from the water, right?
Not really. Having pure water is vital, but apart from the peaty water on Islay there's little flavor given by H_2O.

So it's down to regions then?
Again, not really. Once again, with the exception of Islay, the main impact on a malt's flavor comes from the still and the wood, not *terroir*. It's down to how much (if any) peat has been used, length of ferment is, and the shape and size of the still – the taller the still the more difficult it is for heavily-flavored alcohols to struggle up the pipes, so a lighter, fruitier spirit is made.

Smaller stills make heavier spirit?
In principle yes, but flavor can also depend on how much of the heart is collected. Big whiskies have big hearts; lighter malts tend to have less of the heart collected. There are plenty of tricks a distiller can play – it's down to the people who make it, not the machines they use.

Then put it in barrels and leave it?
Hardly. Up to 60 percent of a malt's flavor comes from the wood. Ex-bourbon barrels give an orangey, coconut flavor, while ex-sherry barrels give clove-like, raisiny notes.

So malts are better than blends?
Not true. You could say that because a blend (which uses grain whisky as well as malt) has more players, it's more complex than a malt. Making blended whisky is an incredible art.

But it's not as complex as wine?
Stick your nose in a glass of malt or a top blended whisky and tell me that. There are just as many flavors and aromas at work in a great dram as there are in a glass of wine. There's a whole new world just waiting...

CELLAR & GLASS

Storing: Whisky doesn't improve in the bottle, but open bottles will oxidize over time, flattening the aroma. Corked whiskies are not uncommon either, so beware!

Serving: 'Do you drink your whisky neat? No, sometimes I like to untuck my shirt...'
Tommy Cooper got it right, sort of. Drink whisky, drink any spirit, in whatever way you want. Adding a little water to whisky releases its aromas and we prefer to drink our top-notch drams this way, but if you want to add cola, soda, ginger or IrnBru then do it!

From peaty to porty

Blended Scotch

Made from a blend of grain whiskies and malts and the reason why Scotch whisky remains such a powerful world player. Still accounts for 90 percent of the Scotch sold in the world. The best are every bit as complex as single malt: the blender's art is an aspect of whisky production that has been disgracefully overlooked. Imagine trying to make a consistent product day in, day out with around 40 different components, all of which are changing constantly. Every cask has a slightly different flavor, and each grain has its own character. We say it's time to rediscover blends – but go for the ones with some age statement on the label; they have the greatest depth and complexity.

Finish

A single malt which has been aged for a long period (usually 12 years or more) in one type of cask (usually ex-bourbon), then decanted and given a short period of ageing in a different type of cask – usually sherry or port. Because the whisky immediately soaks up the residual liquid left in the cask, the final 'finished' product takes on some of its character. Finishes tend to be sweeter than the standard malt, but should always have the character of the distillery showing through.

Grain

The building block for blended Scotch. It is made from wheat or corn and distilled in tall 'column' stills which produce spirit of a much higher strength and lighter character. Each grain distillery has a distinctive character and the quality and flavor of the grain is vitally important in the flavor and complexity of the blend. Occasionally found on its own.

Single Malt

Simple. A malt whisky made from malted barley in one distillery.

Remember, the age on the label is the youngest whisky in the mix. A 12-year-old malt, for example, doesn't mean that as soon as the whisky has its 12th birthday it is pulled out and bottled: there can be 15-, 16-, even 20-year old malts in the bottle adding to the complexity of the final product. Also remember, old doesn't always equal good!

Vatted Malt

A blend (or vatting) of malts from more than one distillery. Most 'regional' supermarket own-labels will be vatted. Nothing wrong with that, but supermarkets have a habit of changing supplier at short notice, so don't be surprised to see that bargain beauty becoming a different beast overnight.

Scotland's are the bravest...?

So whisky is whisky is whisky?

Nothing could be further from the truth. It's made from malted barley, unmalted barley, corn, rye, or wheat. It can be distilled in pot-stills or column stills, aged in new wood in hot climates or used wood in a cool one. We may think that whisky = Scotch, but Ireland, America  (where it's spelt whiskey) Canada... even New Zealand and Bhutan put their own spin on making it. In fact, the Scots copied it from the Irish.

They were the first?

To be honest, no-one can say who made the first spirit of any sort, but it seems likely that Irish monks knew about distillation when the Scots were still painting themselves blue and drinking Pictish heather ale. So why is there more Scotch than Irish, or American? Funny isn't it, that a small, wet country dominates the spirits industry, but things would have been different if Prohibition hadn't happened in America. Obviously it killed off the US industry, but because Ireland relied on the States for its export trade, it went to the wall as well.

So the field's open for Scotch?

Scotland has the most brands (and distilleries) but the quality and choice in world whisky has never been so good. The Irish industry is in top form, making succulent, rounded examples; America is coming back with powerfully-flavored bourbons; there's even increasing interest in Canadian whisky. Flavor is back on the agenda and in spirits that means whisky is on the move again.

Actually, it seems likely that Irish monks knew about distillation when the Scots were still painting themselves blue and drinking Pictish heather ale.

Canada

Dominated by a few huge players making whisky with an easy-going nature. Canadian blenders can use different types of distillation, different mashbills, new or used wood.

Rye whiskey has a citric bite that cracks an old-fashioned whip across palates used to the sweet blandishments of bourbon...

Soft, gentle fruity whiskies that you can take home to meet your mother.

Ireland

The island that gave the world whiskey now only has two distillers; but what results! The key here is not just triple distillation (used by the majority) but use of unmalted barley giving an oily bite. Succulent, peachy and sexy.

Japan

The industry has relied heavily on imported bulk malt from Scotland, even though it's perfectly capable of making great 100 percent Japanese stuff. Self-belief is what's needed.

USA

Bourbon Kentucky bourbon must be made from a 'mashbill' of a minimum of 51 percent corn to which rye (or wheat) and malted barley is added. It must also be aged in new, charred-oak casks. This process gives it a sweet orange-honey character. Big flavors are in vogue and bourbon is on the rise.

Tennessee Tennessee distillers filter the new spirit through beds of maple charcoal to leach out some of the harsher characteristics, and give their whiskey a mellow quality.

Rye Little-seen. A real shame, as rye whiskey has a citric bite that cracks an old-fashioned whip across palates used to the sweet blandishments of bourbon.

Rest of the world

There's decent, sweetish whisky made in Spain, even some in Pakistan, while Indian tends to be a vile mix of bulk Scotch, raw local spirit and lashings of molasses. Thai and Chinese should be left well alone unless you need something to dress a snake bite. There's a malt distillery in Bhutan but, sadly, we haven't been able to try its wares.

Vodka

Not much to say here, surely?

Don't you believe it. Vodka is as fascinating as any other spirit. It's just that its become the mixing spirit that everyone uses and no-one pays any attention to. They think vodka's there just to give a kick to their orange juice, and it's not supposed to taste of anything. The difference between malt whisky and vodka distillers is that the former want to include flavor compounds in the spirit, while vodka distillers want as pure and light a spirit as they can possibly get.

CELLAR & GLASS

Storing: In the freezer – though remember that vodkas under 40% ABV can freeze solid.

Serving: Vodka is like the perfect party hostess. You never notice it but it is somehow always there in the background, giving the mixer a little more confidence, a bit more attitude. Any mixer or fruit juice goes with vodka, but you know that already. The top quality ones (flavored and straight) are, however, best drunk neat and straight from the freezer.

Why?

Vodka originally came from cold countries. Now if you are trying to transport a low-strength spirit in brass monkey weather it will freeze, and that won't do it any good. So distillers needed to make a high-strength spirit, which meant it had to be redistilled. The more you distil the more you remove flavor compounds.

So it doesn't taste of anything?

That's the Zen-like brilliance of it. The greatest vodkas in the world manage to taste clean yet have flavor at the same time. That's purity, not neutrality. You want a kick from rye in Polish and Russian brands, a lush creaminess from potato vodkas, and a soft delicacy from wheat. These flavor and texture differences are what separate the big industrial brands from those from Eastern Europe and Scandinavia. Look: try Wyborowa against Smirnoff Red and see what we're talking about.

Did you say potatoes?

Listen. We won't hear anything against the humble tuber. Just taste Luksusowa and see what the fuss is about. It's all about distillers using what grew around them (or in this case, under them).

OK, I'll drink it neat from now on

Drink it any way you want. Keep it in the freezer, use it to make cocktails, add orange juice or cranberry juice. Vodka is versatile, just remember that the best are fine spirits that can be enjoyed on their own – or in a Martini…

From moonshine to sublime

American

The country which made vodka a global drink has concentrated on making bland – or downright awful – domestic brands. When Russian and Polish vodkas appeared after the end of the Cold War some distillers began to change their ways. The (organic) Rain is perhaps the most interesting.

British

In Britain industrial-style production still rules. Stick to gin or whisky.

Dutch

Every country can make vodka, but Ketel One and Royalty are both great full-flavored pot-still vodkas that prove the worth of Holland.

Flavored

Vodka has been flavored from the word go, but these days it seems as if this tradition has been forgotten with barmen across the world thinking it just means dropping sweeties into the bottle; some cheap imitations use essences. Stick to the classics: Tatra (herbs), Cytrynowka or Limmonaya (lemon peel), Pieprzowka or Stolly Pertsovka (chilli pepper), Krupnik (honey and herbs), Wisniowka (sweet cherry), Zytnia, (rye spirit with apple spirit). Or, our favorite, the mighty beast that is Zubrowka (bison grass).

Polish

The Poles may have been the first nation to produce vodka and, like all distillers, they used native ingredients. Polish vodka tends to be rye-based (Chopin, Krolewska, Wyborowa), or potato-based like Luksusowa. The Poles make the best vodkas in the world. Fact.

Russian

Russian vodka has been the fuel of Russian society from the days of Ivan the Terrible. Wheat and rye have been the chosen raw materials and the best are among the finest in the world: try Altai (wheat), Moskovskaya (rye) and Stolly Cristall (wheat).

Scandinavia and the Baltic

Home to two of the great international brands Absolut (Sweden) and Finlandia (guess). Scandinavian vodka tends to be wheat-based and very pure in character. There are some fine Baltic vodkas appearing from Latvia (Zelta, Rigalya) and Estonia (Eesti Vin, Monopol).

Gin

Ah, mother's ruin!

Gin is so bound up in English culture you tend to forget it's oriGINally Dutch. When English mercenaries went to Holland to fight in the Thirty Years War they found Dutch soldiers drinking 'genever' to settle their nerves (Dutch courage). Soon after, William of Orange became king of Britain, banned imports of brandy and in a spirit of patriotism (or desperation) genever (or gin) became the national English spirit. By the mid-18th century, a fifth of London's houses were distilleries and gin was cheaper than beer. It was the drink of the poor, who drank it in gaudy, mirrored temples to the spirit.

Gilded palaces of gin?

Very clever. Gin fever stopped at the turn of the 19th century when the tax went up, better methods of distillation appeared and rich businessmen like James Burrough, Alexander Gordon, Charles Tanqueray and Felix Booth began to make it. The middle-classes then started drinking their new 'London dry' style, and it took on a different level of popularity altogether.

CELLAR & GLASS

Storing: In the fridge... or the freezer!

Serving: Gin and tonic is a match made in heaven and one of the most mouthwatering mixes of all time, but use small bottles of tonic (they keep their fizz better), make sure the gin is 40% or above, and use lime not lemon. Try gin with lime juice (a Gimlet), Angostura bitters ('pink gin'), or shove sloes or damsons in the bottle and leave to macerate for a few months.

End of story?

Almost. The gin aristocracy blended secret combinations of aromatic spices and peels ('botanicals') and then redistilled them in a high-strength spirit, releasing their aromatic essential oils and giving the gin its distinctive flavor. Juniper gives the main aroma, but coriander seed, orange and lemon peel, cassia and orris root are all used. In that respect, little has changed. The main, scandalous, development has been the recent cutting of strength to below 40% ABV.

So you like a strong drink?

Yes, but something weird happens to gin when it goes below 40%. All the delicate citric aromas disappear and you're left with juniper. You don't just lose strength, you lose flavor and complexity. Now gin, in our minds, is as delicious and fragrant a spirit as any. Please support the best of them, and go for brands that are 40% and above. You know it makes sense.

As English as tuppence, as changeless as canal water

Lithuania

There's a country you didn't expect, but Nemunas is a tremendous, high-strength perfumed brand.

London Dry

A bit of a misnomer these days. It originally meant the new, unsweetened style of gin coming from the middle-class London distillers of the late-1800s. The name stuck, and today you can even find London Dry gin made in Warrington (Bombay, Greenalls, Gloag's), or, in Larios' case, Málaga. There are now only three distilleries making gin in London, the most famous being Beefeater.

Old Tom

The old English style: a juniper spirit sweetened with sugar and glycerine. It's still made for the Finnish market and there's an occasional sighting on shelves in the US.

Genever

The original gin, hailing from the Dutch/Belgian border. It's usually made from rich, pot-still malt spirit and has a much heavier influence of juniper than 'English' gins. It comes in three styles. *Oude* is ripe, heavy and sweet; *jonge* is delicate and clean, and *corenwijn* is aged in cask. All are best drunk ice-cold as chasers.

Plymouth

There's only one distillery in Plymouth and it makes a fantastic, heather and lavender-accented gin that's richer than most London Dry styles. The best? Not far off it.

Spanish

Surprising though it might seem, the Spanish drink a huge amount of gin. Actually, the Spanish drink a huge amount. Much is imported, but the domestically-produced Larios is a good medium-sweet, softly flavored lemony brand.

Brandy

...makes ye randy

Calm down, we're talking about a spirit which could have been the first one of all. If distillation arrived in Europe courtesy of Moorish scholars in southern Spain, then they would have experimented with wine – and brandy, after all, is distilled wine.

So why no brandy in Bordeaux?

Brandy was first made to fortify wine, to make it stable enough to stand long voyages. As maritime trade increased, so more brandy was needed by international traders – specifically the Dutch. It was they who called distilled wine '*brandewijn*' meaning burnt wine, or brandy. They started importing brandy from Cognac and Jerez, for fortification, saw how good it was, and started bottling the stuff.

You didn't answer the question

Why Cognac, not Bordeaux? OK. A good brandy is made from wine that's low in alcohol and high in acidity. The light, tart wines of Cognac and Armagnac are therefore ideal brandy-making stuff. Distil the young wine in a traditional still – no industrial-scale stuff – and then age in barrel, ideally for a long time – up to 20 years will do the trick – and a spirit that is redolent of fruit, spice, nuts, even mushrooms and cheese will appear.

Pricey though?

Sadly true. The finest are beyond the purses of most mortals. One, because they are rare. Two, because it's more expensive to make a bottle of brandy than a bottle of whisky. Grapes cost more than barley.

Drink them neat?

If they are top quality (VSOP and above) then adulteration should be frowned on. More basic VS is great with tonic water or ginger ale.

And does it make you randy?

Pur-leeze!

CELLAR, GLASS & PLATE

Storing: Mostly, the producers have done that for you in oak barrels!

Serving: Try basic VS brandy with tonic water or ginger ale, a tremendous aperitif on a hot day. The adventurous can add lime juice and triple sec (Cointreau) to make a Sidecar.
VSOP and above should be drunk in the classic balloon glass, slowly and alone – that is, no companions in the glass, but as many as you like in the room.

From the unpalatable to the unputdownable

Armagnac
From foie gras territory in the romantic Gascony region of France, armagnac predates cognac by a couple of hundred years. Distilled in tiny column stills at a low strength, it has rich flavors of beech woods, prunes and figs.

Brandy de Jerez
Aged in solera, like sherry (see page 84), the worst are raw spirit, caramel and sherry essence, but the top ones are dark, walnuty and chewy.

Cognac
The world's premier brandy-making region in western France can be broken down into different zones making different styles. Houses blend between subtle, long-ageing Grande Champagne; floral Petite Champagne; waxy, rich Borderies; boisterous early-maturing Fins Bois, and earthy Bons Bois. Distilled twice in pot stills, cognac comes in a baffling range of designations, and prices. All need time to mature, so stick to VSOP quality and above, though if you want the complex fungal, 'rancio' aromas, be prepared to take out a second mortgage.

Fruit brandies
Calvados is the best known, made from apples: 3-Star is industrial stuff, but ancient Hors d'Age standard can be stunning. Good apple brandy is also made in Somerset. *Eaux de vies* from Alsace, Switzerland, Germany and Austria are made by raiding the autumn harvest and distilling every fruit imaginable: try almond-scented Kirsch, delicate Mirabelle, or pure Poire William.

Grappa
Italy makes decent brandy, but this distillation of grape skins (as opposed to juice) is 'clearly' the preferred after-dinner tipple. Cheap ones are vicious firewater, but the finest (cripplingly expensive) grappas are pure essence of the grape.

Pisco
The Peruvians claim to have invented this clear spirit, and you can find some from Bolivia, but Chilean is the most widely exported. Look for Gran Pisco.

Rest of the world
Every winemaking country makes a brandy. Of the rest of them, South Africa's are the highest quality.

Tequila

Slam, bam, thank you ma'am!

Quite. To many, tequila is nothing more than the middle (and interesting) part of the 'slammer' ritual – a lick of salt, a quick shot of neat spirit, and a suck on a wedge of lemon or lime. Refreshing? Even writing about it gets our juices flowing. This is the ultimate party spirit, meant to fuel a wild crowd, preferably in a hip Tex-Mex bar. You'll love a tequila slammer or six that night, and loathe your hangover the next morning.

A bad case of tequila sunrise?

After a night on the slammers, you bet. But there's much more to tequila than this. And we don't just mean the Margarita, fine cocktail though it is. This is an underrated drink. Trade up to serious, barrel-aged tequila and discover a fine, complex, 'sipping' spirit. Rule of thumb: buy young white tequila for slammers, either white or gold tequila for cocktails, and *reposado* or *añejo* tequila for swirling round a tumbler and savoring, like a fine brandy or whisky.

What ami-goes into it?

It's made in Mexico from the large, fleshy agave plant, a member of the lily family. Blue agaves (the best sort) take eight to 12 years to reach maturity. When they're harvested, the pineapple-like heart of the plant is steamed and crushed to produce a sweet juice, which is fermented and distilled. The clear spirit is either bottled straight away, or aged in oak barrels. Great brands include the ubiquitous José Cuervo, plus Porfidio, Tres Magueyes, Real Hacienda and El Tesoro.

A worm wriggles into every bottle?

No, gringo! Worms are often found in mezcal – which can be made from any sort of agave plant all over Mexico. Tequila is subject to stricter quality controls, and is produced in only one small region of the country (around Tequila town – it's just like cognac production being centred around, er, Cognac) from at least 51 percent blue agave spirit. Tequila tends to be more expensive, and finer, than mezcal. And it's wormless. Mezcal can be an astoundingly rough industrial spirit, but worm-free brands such as Hacienda Sotol and Del Maguey prove that in the right hands it can be as good as tequila. The worm, incidentally, won't get you high – it's just a gimmick. A revolting one.

From the slammer to the emergency room

Joven
(aka white, or silver tequila)

The clear, peppery spirit frequently knocked back in slammers. It's bottled young ('*joven*'), and tastes relatively simple, perhaps with a fresh, grassy aroma and note of citrus fruit.

Gold

Young tequila that has acquired a slightly sweeter, more mellow flavor from the addition of caramel. Not as good as the barrel-aged stuff, but a decent component in cocktails.

Reposado

Meaning 'rested' – in oak barrels. Tequilas labelled *reposado* are barrel-matured for between two and 11 months. The oak adds intricate layers of flavor – look out for a spicy, toffeed hint. Drink *reposado* tequila on its own (and on your own, or at least away from the Club 18-30 crowds) – it deserves it.

Anejo

Aged tequila – it has spent over a year in cask. Notes from a recent tequila tasting (it's hard to remember the actual event) reveal intriguing notes of over-ripe pear, chocolate, vanilla, coffee, spice and herbs in a line-up of fine *anejos*. Don't be conned by *anejos* that have spent years and years in barrel – the relatively delicate tequila spirit can't take too much wood. Let the blue agave shine through!

100 percent blue agave

Made in any of the above styles, these are the best tequilas, produced from pure blue agave juice. Prices are set to soar over the next few years as an agave disease and poor cross-breeding, plus a destructive pesky weevil, have all drastically reduced the crop. At the same time, demand has risen sharply since the Latino bar scene became seriously cool and began to show a preference for this fine tequila.

Rum

Brown Sugar... you taste so good!

Spot on! We love rum. We think it is undervalued, unappreciated, overlooked and forgotten. It's more than just glasses of thick black stuff knocked back by fishermen or retired admirals. It's a versatile and flavorsome spirit that comes in different styles, is made in different ways, makes a mean cocktail and just puts a smile on your face. Not bad for a by-product.

That's a bit cruel, isn't it?

Hey, all spirits started out as by-products of some agricultural crop, in rum's case it was sugar cane. Without sugar cane there could be no rum, but without the slave trade there would have been no sugar cane. All spirits have their secrets, but rum's is more bloodstained than most.

How is it made?

In one of two ways. Either by using molasses – the method preferred in the 'British' West Indies, or fermented sugar cane – used in the French Antilles, Haiti and Brazil. The latter method gives a floral, aromatic lift. Both types can either be distilled in pot stills, giving a rich character, or column stills, which make a slightly lighter style.

So what about white, gold & dark?

White rum is unaged. Try out the high-strength Overproof with its creamy, oily richness. Gold rums get their color from cask-ageing, which can be anything from 12 months to 21 years. They start off with banana cream notes, then, as they age, so crème brûlée, toffee, orange, toast, nutmeg and pulpy fruit all begin to appear. Because the Caribbean is hot and humid, the rum extracts a lot of flavor and woodiness from the cask, so many British firms age rums in the cooler climes of Leith or Bristol. These dark rums are a blend from different islands and often have large dollops of caramel added to them.

CELLAR & GLASS

Storing: As long as you like!

Serving: Rum is the foundation of the Daiquiri and is another spirit that positively springs into life in the presence of lime juice. When making a rum punch remember the golden rule: 'Sour, sweet, strong and weak.' In other words, use lime juice or bitters; fruit (syrup, juice, grenadine); rum, and ice or water.

Hello sailor...rum chums

Australia

Well, what did you think Bundaberg was? All the way from the cane fields of Queensland to the toilet bowls of Earl's Court. Joke! We love it dearly. Well... like it.

Bacardi

Made across the globe, it dominates its world like no other spirit. Now cynically trying to reclaim its long-lost Cuban heritage. Bland and boring. We don't like it. And that's no joke!

Barbados

Top-class rums are made on Barbados, particularly the soft, elegant aged gold from Mount Gay and Cockspur. Mellowest you'll ever find!

Brazil

Cachaça, the spirit behind the Caipirinha, is a sugar cane rum. Some is evil enough to fuel a São Paulo bus, but Ypioca and <51> are good.

Britain

Most 'British' rums are thick, black and sweet, but check out the aged rums from Cadenhead and Bristol Brandy to see just how good the UK's can be.

Cuba

Bacardi fled with Batista, leaving the Cubans to continue the Havana Club tradition: it's an aromatic, elegant rum that's great at three years old, superb at seven and unbelievable at 15.

Guadeloupe

The French-Caribbean *département* makes *rhum* from sugar cane, not molasses, distils in Armagnac-style stills and produces perfumed, spicy spirits that age superbly.

Guyana

Massive rum producer, mainly making full-flavored blending rums for British, American and German markets. Try the complex El Dorado. Superb!

Haiti

Only one commercial distiller here (Barbancourt), but what Haiti lacks in numbers it makes up for in quality. An absolutely cracking, complex *rhum*.

Jamaica

Though traditionally Jamaica has made the most robust rums of all, a huge range is available, from the definitive Overproof (Wray & Nephew) to the smoky, aged Appleton Estate.

Martinique

Like Guadeloupe, the best are complex, aged spirits. Dillon, Bally and JM are the top producers.

Trinidad

Massive distilleries can make any kind of rum you want, including the amazingly strong Stallion or clean, soft, golden Ferdi.

Other spirits

Weird alchemy

Ever since some unknown ancient discovered the art of distillation, people have been making spirits from all manner of ingredients. In the earliest days of distillation alchemists, in their vain attempts to distil the essence of the stuff of life itself (by the way, this is the 'gold' they are always pictured trying to make), used anything they could get their hands on – one recipe calls for human brains and horse shit, another for swan, yet another for crushed pearls. That strangeness apart, the earliest distillers were monks who were less interested in the alcoholic effects of their spirits than in their healing properties (well, that's their story and they're sticking to it). They used the folk medicine ingredients of their time – roots, berries, grasses, herbs, peels – and redistilled them to produce elixirs, apparently magical potions that could be used to cure every ailment known to man. You could say, therefore, that liqueurs were the first spirits of all, though they weren't sipped after dinner along with the Ferrero-Rocher chocolates but were used to treat bubonic plague, scurvy, gangrene and all manner of pestilential and pustulent diseases.

Drinks of the past?

You can still find them, actually. Chartreuse, the greatest liqueur of all, is still made to an ancient recipe which not only lays down which herbs and roots to use but also prescribes at which phase of the moon they should be harvested. Absinthe – the great spirit that enraptured Rimbaud and Baudelaire and which has recently been rediscovered by louche inhabitants of inner London – first appeared on top of the stove of a pair of weird sisters in the Alps. They used local ingredients (including the all-important wormwood) to make a cure-all medicine. Juniper berries (the main ingredient in gin) were first distilled to try and find a cure for the plague. Bitters are still used as digestive aids – Angostura was invented as a cure for malaria. It was really only in the 19th century that liqueurs stopped becoming liquids you drank to make yourself feel better and became sweet after-dinner tipples.

Legends or leg-pulls?

Strangely, around the same time, a host of 'secret' recipes also sprang into being. No liqueur is worth its salt if it doesn't have a secret recipe, a monk, or a plucky servant girl to give it some sort of dubious heritage and credibility. If Baileys had been invented at that time, no doubt someone would have 'found' a legend of a mythical Irish cow which gave its milk willingly to produce a drink fit for heroes. Liqueurs don't really need these stories. The best are great drinks which balance sweetness with a herbal, sometimes bitter, bite and they show the craft and care that distillers have used for centuries. Be prepared for a taste of the peculiar.

That's the spirit

Absinthe

Made from spirit redistilled with star anise, herbs and wormwood. So much of this high-strength spirit was drunk that the French authorities banned it. Now it's being revived and there's a raft of badly-made 'absinthes' cashing-in on its wild reputation.

Advocaat

Truly horrible gloopy egg-yolk liqueur. Avoid at all costs.

Anise

Drunk throughout the Mediterranean. Each country has its own variant on spirit flavored with star anise. Pastis is what French absinthe producers began making after absinthe was banned. Pernod is sweet, Ricard drier, but Janot is the best and most traditional. Ouzo and raki are drier. Very refreshing, they're great with mezze. We adore Spanish pacharan, a heady, sweet anise spirit macerated with sloes. Italy's sambuca is thicker.

Bitters

Originally an aid to digestion, the most bitter – Fernet-Branca, Underberg – are great hangover cures; Averna and Gammeldansk are softer and sweeter, while Suze, the bitter orange beauty of Campari, and even the explosive Jagermeister, are 'session' drinks. No home should be without flavor-packed Angostura bitters, but try to find aromatic Peychaud bitters as well.

Liqueurs

Cream Strangely popular invention. Like mildly alcoholic ice-cream.

Fruit Orange peel is used for sweet, tingly Cointreau, herbal Ponche and the complex, tangy Grand Marnier, while the floaty aromas of Mandarine Napoleon come from tangerine. Lemon peel is pressed into service for Italy's Limoncello, while cherries are behind the intense sweet/sour Luxardo and silky Cherry Heering.

Herbs First made as medicines with huge numbers of healing herbs, this is the secretive branch of spirits. The best is the amazingly complex Chartreuse, then comes herbal, sweet Benedictine. Strega and Galliano are simpler.

Nuts Amaretto's famous marzipan aromas are from crushed almond and apricot seeds. Nocello is softer, sweeter. Caraway seeds are used in dry, bitter kummel and sticky goldwasser.

Zytnia

Well we had to have a 'Z'. It's a wonderful Polish rye vodka by the way.

Fruit spirit flavor tree

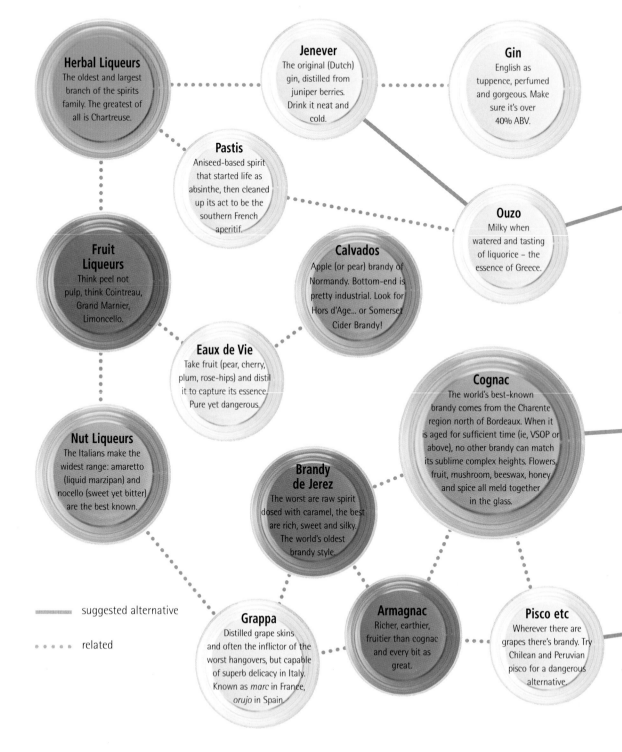

Herbal Liqueurs
The oldest and largest branch of the spirits family. The greatest of all is Chartreuse.

Jenever
The original (Dutch) gin, distilled from juniper berries. Drink it neat and cold.

Gin
English as tuppence, perfumed and gorgeous. Make sure it's over 40% ABV.

Pastis
Aniseed-based spirit that started life as absinthe, then cleaned up its act to be the southern French aperitif.

Fruit Liqueurs
Think peel not pulp, think Cointreau, Grand Marnier, Limoncello.

Calvados
Apple (or pear) brandy of Normandy. Bottom-end is pretty industrial. Look for Hors d'Age... or Somerset Cider Brandy!

Ouzo
Milky when watered and tasting of liquorice – the essence of Greece.

Eaux de Vie
Take fruit (pear, cherry, plum, rose-hips) and distil it to capture its essence. Pure yet dangerous.

Cognac
The world's best-known brandy comes from the Charente region north of Bordeaux. When it is aged for sufficient time (ie, VSOP or above), no other brandy can match its sublime complex heights. Flowers, fruit, mushroom, beeswax, honey and spice all meld together in the glass.

Nut Liqueurs
The Italians make the widest range: amaretto (liquid marzipan) and nocello (sweet yet bitter) are the best known.

Brandy de Jerez
The worst are raw spirit dosed with caramel, the best are rich, sweet and silky. The world's oldest brandy style.

Grappa
Distilled grape skins and often the inflictor of the worst hangovers, but capable of superb delicacy in Italy. Known as *marc* in France, *orujo* in Spain.

Armagnac
Richer, earthier, fruitier than cognac and every bit as great.

Pisco etc
Wherever there are grapes there's brandy. Try Chilean and Peruvian pisco for a dangerous alternative.

suggested alternative

••••• related

Vegetable spirit flavor tree

Tequila
Contrary to popular belief, tequila is NOT made from cactus, but agave – look for 100 percent blue agave on the label. These are delicate, complex spirits with aromas of pear and decadently rotting fruit. A truly great drink.

Mezcal
Does NOT make you trip. The best are every bit as good and complex as fine tequila.

.... suggested alternative

· · · · · related

Potato Vodka
Well it's a vegetable isn't it? Polish speciality and wonderfully creamy it is too.

Dark
British speciality. Thick, concentrated rum, almost singed around the edges.

Gold
Aged in casks. Alcoholic banana split with extra elegance. Mount Gay, Appleton, Havana Club. Gorgeous stuff.

Rhum
French variant made from sugar cane, not molasses. Lighter and more perfumed.

Rum
Rum was a by-product of the slave trade, but has now become a proud distillation of all that's great about the Caribbean. Every island has its own spin on things, from the rich and heavy Jamaican pot-still, fragrant rums of Barbados, to the delicate rhums from Guadeloupe, and perfumed rums from Cuba. The spirit world's most ignored classic.

White
Light and often neutral and boring (think Bacardi). Go for Overproof.

Cachaça
Brazil's own rum. Mix with lime for a refreshing 'Caipirinha'.

Grain spirit flavor tree

Japanese
No longer a Scotch imitation. Lighter but with a racy style.

Bourbon
Think vanilla, hickory, orange peel and lemon. Sweet but powerful and behind the world's greatest cocktail: the Manhattan.

Canadian
Corn-based, soft, gentle, sweet, but NOT boring.

Irish
Made from malted and unmalted barley. Softer, juicier and fruitier than Scotch.

Whisky
Originally a Celtic spirit made from surplus grain and now the world's best-known spirit. Scotland may lead the way in volume, but don't dismiss the world's other examples.

Rye
Isn't Canadian whisky but an American speciality. Oily, citric with a whiplash of zesty flavor. Hard core stuff.

Malt
Made from malted barley, water and yeast. That's it! Mysterious, complex, fascinating.

Grain
Made from wheat (or corn) distilled to high strength. When mixed with malt produces blended Scotch.

Jenever
Dutch gin is traditionally made from malt spirit redistilled with juniper berries.

Gin
In Britain it's made from a grain whisky that's been redistilled to a high strength and then distilled again with botanicals.

Korn/schnapps
German grain spirit, often flavored. (Austrian schnapps is an eaux-de-vie by the way.)

━━━━━━ suggested alternative

• • • • • related

Wheat Vodkas
The most gentle of the vodka styles, wheat is the preferred grain in the Scandinavian and Baltic countries.

Rye Vodkas
Mainly a Russian/Polish style with a zesty bite to them.

Potato Vodkas
Don't think potato = horrible hooch, Polish potato vodka is lusciously creamy and smooth. Look for Luksusowa or Baltic. Gorgeous stuff!

Vodka
Most people don't give vodka a second thought. After all, it's a spirit that is there to be mixed, isn't it? The greatest examples, however, are spirits which manage to achieve a strange Zen-like balance of being a drink that's totally pure yet still has flavor. Neutrality is a bad thing in vodka: instead it should taste delicate, ethereal, clean and have traces of the grain it is made from.

Neutral Spirit Vodkas
Dreadful Westernised imitations of the real thing. Use instead of petrol.

Flavored Vodkas
These aren't a new development. Vodkas have had herbs, spices and fruit macerated in them since they first appeared and some are among the most sophisticatedly flavored spirits in the world.

Akvavit
Norwegian/Danish grain spirit, sometimes flavored with caraway. Drink ice cold and frequently.

Fruit Vodkas
New-style flavored vodkas use artificial essences. Old-style, like Polish Wisniowska (cherry) or Cytronowka (lemon) use real fruit and have beautifully pure aromas.

Herbs & Spices
Once made as medicine or as a tipple for frozen hunters, these are vodkas flavored with up to 35 herbs and spices. The greatest, Zubrowka, uses just one – bison grass.

Kummel
Caraway-flavored Baltic speciality, and beloved by flatulent golfers in Surrey.

Aged
Not that common admittedly but both Russia and Poland make cask-aged versions called *starka* which can also have herbs and spices added to them.

Cocktails

If style **gurus** are to be believed, we are entering a new cocktail era. Bars are beginning to take over from pubs, bartenders are now calling themselves **'mixologists'** and cocktail shakers are once more being wielded with **glee**. The Martini is being drunk once more and old stagers like the Manhattan, Bellini and Cosmopolitan have undergone a welcome **revival**. It's all part of drinkers rediscovering quality, flavor and a sense of adventure! But what happens when your friends all want to be served some **exotic** wonder? Don't panic, cocktails are a hell of a lot easier to master than you'd **believe.**

In the mix

It strikes us that cocktails were probably accidentally invented on a rainy Wednesday afternoon in New York in the 1820s by some bored barkeep who decided to relieve the tedium by mixing a number of spirits to see what happened. The same thing still goes on – Dave well recalls the Jack Daniel's and coconut milk foisted on him at 4am by a friend convinced he'd created a masterpiece. Some combinations work, others... well...even Picasso had the odd off day.

Get spinning

Cocktails are fluid creations in every sense. They are jam sessions for bar-men – psychedelic-hued, jazz-tinged improvisations with spirits, shaker and ice. The arcane terminology, the flashy pouring, shaking and assembling looks complex, and is a great art, but in essence, cocktails are simple creations. A Martini, which is at the root of most of the modern classics, has a Zen-like simplicity to it, but getting it right is perhaps the bartender's greatest test.

Less is more

Take a look at any classic cocktail (old or new) and you can see that very few have a mass of ingredients; rather they are about a subtle melding and shifting of flavor. The essence is to hit a balance so that no ingredient dominates. The main flavor, which is given by the base spirit, is then transported to another plane by the addition of a second (or third) spirit and then flavored and lifted with a drop of bitters, a splash of colored liqueur, or a squeeze of lime.

Talking 'bout my generation

Every generation rediscovers the cocktail. What started out as drinks for the elite in grand American hotels, became the fuel for the Roaring Twenties, gave us the three-Martini lunch, reappeared as the fluffy pink liquid inspiration for disco, and are now being reinterpreted as ironic, post-modern drinks. Cocktails are like rock 'n roll. Nothing is 100 percent new; riffs can be traced back to blind bluesmen and wild hillbilly preachers. Today's are just a new spin on the basics: part of the rediscovery of flavor which has fuelled people's new-found passion for wine and beer.

Crystal clear tips

You don't need to stock up on every bizarre liqueur in the world. It's amazing what can be done with your kitchen equipment, a bottle of spirits, vermouth, fruit juice, ice and limes!

Here are some tips – and terminology... Shaking: it mixes the ingredients, chills the drink down and lightly dilutes it. Shakers should never be more than half-filled with ice and you needn't shake for longer than 10 seconds. Then strain the contents so that none of the ice ends up in the drink. You can also use the shaker for stirring (again over ice cubes). Both are equally valid, it just depends on how much dilution you like in your drink. Shaking is best for ingredients that don't go together so well, while stirring is used for those which marry easily, but you choose. Dave likes his Manhattans stirred, Susy shakes 'em. Oh, and a clean sealed jar works just as well! Some recipes call for muddling, which is mushing the ingredients, usually fruit, mint and sugar, in the bottom of a glass with a pestle or the back of a spoon. And remember the ice. Chlorinated water has the same effect on a cocktail as cork taint has on a wine – use bottled water.

The recipe for success...

Note, all measurements here are metric (30ml=1oz, or two and a half tablespoons). A dash is a mere drip, while a splash is a little more. And buy quality spirits – you can't make a good cocktail with crap ingredients!

Classics

Dave's Bloody Mary
50ml Pieprzowka/Absolut Peppar
ice
In jug combine:
tomato juice
Worcestershire sauce
white pepper
salt
dash of celery salt
splash of fresh lime juice
splash of chilled manzanilla sherry
Tabasco sauce to taste
Pour mix over vodka. Stir. Drink.
Begin to feel better.
TIP: Make the mix the night
before; store in the fridge. And
make plenty of it.

Caipirinha
1 lime, quartered
1 tsp sugar syrup
50ml cachaça (or white rum)
Put lime and syrup in bottom of
large tumbler (highball glass).
Muddle well for a minute to extract
juice and lime oil. Add ice. Stir. Add
cachaca. Stir again. Add soda to
make it long.
TRY THIS! Make a caipirinha with
Absolut Mandarin and fresh
mandarins/tangerines.

Champagne Cocktail
1 sugar cube
dash Angostura bitters
10ml brandy
Champagne
Place sugar cube into Champagne
flute and dash with Angostura. Pour
in brandy and Champagne.

Cosmopolitan
50ml vodka
30ml Cointreau
15ml lime juice
splash cranberry juice
lime twist
Stir and strain into a chilled cocktail
glass with sugared rim. Garnish with
a lime twist.
TIP: To sugar (or salt) the rim, don't
bury the rim in a pile of salt. Moisten
the rim with lime juice and turn the
glass side-on in a saucer of sugar
(or salt).

Daiquiri
50ml white rum
juice of 1 lime
1 tsp sugar
Shake over ice into cocktail glass.
Frozen Daiquiri
As above, plus any fruit. Zap in
blender with crushed ice.

Gin Fizz
30ml lemon juice
10ml simple syrup
  (see Mint Julep for method)
1 tsp sugar
60ml gin
soda
Shake the first four, strain into tall
glass filled with ice cubes. Add soda.
Try this with any spirit.

Manhattan
50ml bourbon
30ml sweet vermouth
3 dashes Angostura bitters
drop maraschino juice
maraschino cherry
Stir over ice in mixing glass. Strain
and garnish with cherry.
Substitute Cointreau for vermouth
and you have an Uptown Manhattan.

Margarita
50ml tequila
30ml Cointreau
60ml fresh lime
Shake and strain into salt-rimmed
glass.
TIP: Try Maldon salt for a
spectacular effect. Because it's made
of salt flakes the rim looks like it's
topped with shards of glass. Crazy,
man!

*30ml = 1 oz, or 2 1/2 Tablespoons

Classic Martini

1 tsp Noilly Prat

90ml gin

twist of lemon

*Shake vermouth in shaker with ice.
Strain. Add gin into shaker. Stir and
strain. Add lemon twist. Serve in
cocktail glass.*

Mint Julep

90ml bourbon

30ml simple syrup

3 cups crushed ice

6 sprigs mint

*Pack two-thirds of a tall glass
with ice. Add bourbon and syrup.
Stir. Pack more ice on top so it domes
over the top. Garnish with mint
and wait until a film of ice forms
on the glass.*

*TIP: To make simple syrup take equal
parts sugar and water, bring to a
gentle simmer until sugar has fully
dissolved. Cool and refrigerate.
Simple!*

Mojito

fresh mint leaves

1 tsp simple sugar syrup (as above)

half a lime

50ml Havana Club

soda water

sprig of mint

*In large highball glass 'muddle' the
mint and sugar syrup. Squeeze juice
from lime into glass and add lime
half. Add rum and ice. Stir. Add
soda water. Stir briefly and garnish
with mint.*

*TIP: To get the authentic Havana
experience don't wash the mint.*

Old Fashioned

½ tsp simple sugar syrup

splash water

3 dashes Angostura bitters

half orange wheel

maraschino cherry

75ml bourbon

*In highball glass muddle the sugar
syrup, water, bitters, orange and
cherry, lightly mushing up the fruit.
Fill the glass with ice cubes and add
bourbon. Stir.*

Piña Colada

crushed ice

30ml Appleton Special/Overproof rum

50ml unsweetened pineapple juice

20ml coconut cream

15ml Appleton 12-year-old

*Blend ice, white rum, juice and cream
and pour into a tall glass. Top up
with the 12-year-old rum.*

Susy's Pisco Sour

50ml pisco

30ml lime juice

3 tsps simple sugar syrup

1 tbsp lightly whipped egg white

ice cube

2 dashes Angostura bitters

*Pour all ingredients except bitters
into shaker. Shake and strain into
highball glass. Add bitters.*

Tequila Sunrise

lime

50ml tequila

100ml orange juice

2 dashes grenadine

*Squeeze lime over ice into large
highball glass. Add tequila and
orange juice, then pour in grenadine.*

The Seelbach Cocktail
(The Seelbach Hotel, Louisville, KY)

30ml bourbon

20ml Cointreau

7 dashes Angostura bitters

7 dashes Peychaud bitters

150ml Champagne

orange twist

*Put bourbon, Cointreau and bitters
in Champagne flute and stir. Add
Champagne and twist.*

*Peychaud bitters are slightly sweeter
than Angostura and have a touch of
anise and orange about them.*

Modern classics

Attitude Adjuster
(Anita, Tin Drum, Brighton)

half a lime
20ml white rum
20ml gin
20ml vodka
20ml tequila
10ml triple sec
sparkling wine

Squeeze lime into a tall glass, add ice cubes and spirits. Stir and top up with sparkling wine.
TIP: Use cola instead of wine for a Long Island Iced Tea, or cranberry for a New England Iced Tea.

Bombay Bellini

puréed fresh mango
dash lemon juice
dash peach brandy
sparkling wine

Stir juice and brandy in a Champagne flute. Top up with sparkling wine.

*30ml = 1 oz, or 2 1/2 Tablespoons

Centenario

40ml gold rum
30ml Overproof white rum
10ml Kahlua
10ml Cointreau
juice of 1 lime
mint sprig
dash grenadine

Stir ingredients over ice in a tall glass.

Dangerous Currants

50ml Wyborowa vodka
10ml crème de cassis
tonic water
wedge of lime

Half-fill tall glass with ice cubes. Add vodka and cassis. Stir. Top up with tonic and garnish with the lime.

Golden Eye

40ml Wyborowa vodka
20ml Goldschlager
Brut Champagne

Pour vodka and Goldschlager into flute. Add Champagne.

Havana Laugh
(Drey, Brown's, Brighton)

40ml Havana Club 3-year-old
15ml Peach schnapps
30ml puréed strawberry
50ml pineapple juice
dash lemon juice
teaspoon sugar
6–8 basil leaves

Shake all ingredients. Strain into highball glass.

Havana Mandarin
(Alastair Sollis, Duke of Cambridge, Oxford)

6 kumquats
1 lime
25 ml honey syrup
dash orange bitters
50 ml Havana Club 3-year-old
Splash Mandarin Napoleon

Halve the kumquats and quarter the lime and muddle in a tall glass with the honey syrup and bitters. Add ice, Havana Club. Stir. Float Mandarin Napoleon on top. Garnish with mint.

Longshot
(Adam Seger, The Seelbach, Louisville, Kentucky)
50ml bourbon
15ml ginger liqueur
15ml peach schnapps
Shake and serve in cocktail glass. Garnish with crystallised ginger.

Mandarin Martini
splash Mandarin Napoleon
dash Cointreau
40ml gin
15ml vodka
mandarin twist
Pour liqueurs in empty shaker. Coat and discard surplus. Add ice and other ingredients. Shake and strain into cocktail glass. Garnish with twist.

Martini Thyme
80ml gin
25ml Green Chartreuse
1 sprig of thyme
Stir together the gin and Chartreuse. Strain into cocktail glass and garnish with thyme.

Metropolitan
50ml Absolut Kurant
15ml Rose's lime cordial
15ml lime juice
30ml cranberry juice
lime wedge to garnish
Shake and strain into cocktail glass and garnish with the wedge of lime.

Molotov Cocktail
80ml Finlandia vodka
15ml Woodford Reserve bourbon
15ml Café Sambuca
Shake and strain into cocktail glasses. Flame.

Under the Volcano
(Dave)
30ml Chicicapa Mezcal
15ml Overproof white rum
10ml Cointreau
lime juice
lime twist
Shake and serve in cocktail glass and garnish with the twist. Throw dead dog into ravine after it.

Sea Breeze
50ml Wyborowa vodka
50ml cranberry juice
30ml grapefruit juice
Shake and strain into highball glass. TIP: Great party drink. Make it up in jugs.

Where The Buffalo Roam
dash Chambéry
50ml Wyborowa
15ml Zubrowka
blade of bison grass
Coat shaker with Chambéry and discard excess. Add ice, vodka and shake. Garnish with blade of grass.

Woo Woo
40ml peach schnapps
40ml vodka
100ml cranberry juice
Pour all ingredients into a highball glass over ice cubes, stir, and serve. TIP: Jugs of this can be made in advance. Perfect for parties.

Party fuel

The **eleventh** commandment: 'Thou shall not provide crap drink to thy neighbor'. Get the booze right, and your **party** will **swing** (regardless of the fact your music is terrible and no one interesting turns up). Here, then, is the **essential** low-down on the rights and wrongs of party drinks, and, in case you're **cooking** too, we've listed the food and wine matches made in **heaven**. Praise be!

Party politics

Party Fears, One:

Most people don't think very hard about what to serve at a drinks party. It's simple to put out a few bottles of uninspiring warmish white – chances are no one will actually complain. But party drinks can be much, much more interesting than that. In this chapter we tell you how easy it is to come up with delicious wines, beers and spirits to fuel a crowd. And how you don't have to spend a fortune to do it.

Here's the low-down on which styles of inexpensive wine (white, red and sparkling) go down best at parties. Why it's important to serve all of them cold, and how to achieve this even when it's 90 degrees outside... Which spirits are the best bet, and how to pick more exciting beers than usual... And how to mop up a red wine spillage, and cope with a lost corkscrew. The idea is that if you plan your party well, you can enjoy a hassle-free night, knowing your guests are guzzling decent grog.

Party Fears, Two:

If you think spilt wine is a sticky problem, try food and wine matching. Let's not get too prescriptive here, as most bottles are reasonably OK with most dishes. But it's also true that a few food and wine partnerships are fantastically good, while a few others create a horrible clash of flavor or texture.

The key is to dismiss those strict, boring, old-fashioned rules (like always pairing white wine with fish, and red wine with meat), and instead take on board some general guidelines. Above all, it's important to match food and wine partners which have similar levels of acidity, sweetness, intensity of flavor and tannin.

So, if you're serving a tart, acidic dish (tomato salad and vinaigrette, say) you will have more luck with a crisp, tangy dry white than a rich, oaky, low acid one. Very sweet puds, like treacle tart, demand almost cloying, rich, unctuous wines, while lighter fruit

salads need more delicate, crisper, sweet styles. And concentrated, tannic reds work very well with hearty stews and tough red meat, breaking down the protein in the mouth, but they clash with mild, simple fare.

Another clever trick is to work out which sauces, or flavorings, match your food (eg, lemon with fish, redcurrant with lamb) and find a wine which has similar characteristics (in this case, say, Sancerre with the fish, Merlot with the lamb). This even works for some less obvious condiments, like herbs, mint or pepper, as some wines really do have hints of these flavors.

On page 140 we've listed the best food and wine matches of all time. We've gone for the most enduring, ever-popular marriages – the classics of food and wine matching – rather than trendy, flash-in-the-pan affairs. We're talking Bogie and Bacall here, not Patsy and Liam.

It's my party

Choosing your drinks

Q: Should I go mainly for white wine?

A: Yes – at a drinks party. Whites are usually lighter, more refreshing and thirst-quenching than red, so they are in demand more. Cater for two-thirds white to one-third red. If it's a dinner or lunch party balance it out 50:50.

Q: There are so many different styles of white wine around. Which ones are best for parties?

A: Avoid very rich whites, or sweeter styles, or the sort of heavily-oaked Chardonnays that only appeal to termites. These wines have their moments (with food, usually), but they make lousy *apéritifs*. That said, don't go for whites with mouth-puckering acidity, as dry as the Gobi Desert. A little soft, sunny fruit flavor won't go amiss. Choose good-quality South African Chenin Blanc, Pinot Gris (or a premium Pinot Grigio), youthful, unoaked Aussie Chardonnay, New World Riesling, or aromatic Sauvignon Blanc from New Zealand.

Q: What about reds?

A: Don't pick a too-serious, heavy, tannic red. If it's got to slip down easily without food, you'll need a reasonably light-bodied red with ripe berry flavors and a smooth texture. Do choose: Beaujolais (making sure you avoid the very cheapest), young French Pinot Noir, or juicy Chilean Merlot. Southern Italy and Portugal produce many bargain, easy-drinking reds these days, so try these too.

Q: Any other wines I could wave under my friends' noses?

A: Try a trio of Spanish wines: Cava (good-value sparkling wine), bone-dry fino or manzanilla sherry (incredibly refreshing – serve well-chilled), and in summer, fruity, bright *rosado*, again served cold.

Q: Volume?

A: You know your friends. But catering for a bottle of wine per head isn't as mad or hedonistic as it sounds. Basically, you can't buy too much (not if you buy your drink sale or return). But you can definitely buy too little. Happens all the time.

Q: What about beer?

A: Of course. Bottles, please, not cans (which look cheap). Light continental

lagers go down well at parties. Then there are fruit beers and wheat/white beers, which show more imagination than big-brand lagers. And they're particularly refreshing. Tip: beer in smaller bottles remains cold all the way down, so go for the little bottles if you really want to stay cool.

Q: And spirits?

A: Spirits can be a drag for the host, who has to provide mixers and ice, and quite possibly make up the drinks all night. If you want blithe spirits, mix huge jugfuls of the simplest cocktails: Margaritas, Caiparinhas, Woo Woos, or Bellinis – all dead easy (see pages 132–135).

Q: How do I keep all these drinks cool?

A: Warm wine or beer is nasty, especially at a hot, crowded party. Chill all wines and beers mentioned above fairly hard (harder than you would do at any other time), except the reds, which still benefit from half an hour's light chilling. To avoid the fridge bursting, fill the bath with tons of ice (relatively cheap stuff) and keep the bottles in there, or use a big, clean, plastic tub or bin instead. Or, unless it's positively balmy, put the bottles outside in the garden or on the balcony and raid your stock now and again.

Q: What really works for red wine stains?

A: Two ways to minimize the damage done by spilt red wine. First, soak up the excess by pressing hard with an old towel, then chuck a load of salt on the mess and wait till morning when it has been absorbed and dried. Then vacuum up the pink salt castle – the remaining damage should be minimal. Second, follow the red wine with a good soaking of white – it really does counteract it.

Q: Anything else to ensure we all have a good time – including me, of course?

A: Here's a check-list:
(1) Losing the corkscrew is a total pain. Invest in a couple of extras – the simple 'waiter's friend' type is inexpensive. Or buy wine in screw-cap bottles for convenience (tread carefully, some screw-capped wines are vile).
(2) Provide appealing soft drinks for the drivers – cranberry juice or elderflower pressé go down better than plain water or orange juice.
(3) Put out several ashtrays.
(4) Stock-pile bin liners, paper napkins, toilet roll, salt and old towels (see above), plus bread, coffee and Dave's Bloody Mary Mix for morning-after hangers-on and hangovers.
(5) Buy booze on a sale or return basis.
(6) Hire glasses from your wine shop, and enquire about ice there.
(7) Put a list of cab numbers by the phone, and simply point at it when guests need a lift home.

Food matching

FOOD	WINE/DRINK	WHY DOES IT WORK?
Beef – plain roast or grilled steak	Argentinean Malbec, Australian Shiraz, Châteauneuf-du-Pape	Rich, ripe fruit, plenty of concentrated flavor, and firm but distinctly rounded tannins are called for
Cheese – mild & soft	Sancerre goes brilliantly with goat's cheese (chèvre) and pretty well with Brie and Camembert	Why? Tannins will clash; high acidity is needed to cut through the gorgeous fat
Cheese – blue	Sweet styles. Drink tawny port or malmsey Madeira with Stilton, while Sauternes or Barsac with Roquefort is unbeatable. Monbazillac is a cheaper option	Sweetness is a good foil for the saltiness of blue cheese. The nutty flavor of tawny port and Madeira suits cheese as does a handful of nuts
Cheese – strong, hard	Rioja gran reserva, or a mature red from Ribera del Duero. Strong southern French reds work well too	You need some oomph and power here – a savory, herbal, even spicy note
Chicken or turkey, and all the trimmings	Lightish white burgundy – a good Chablis is fabulous. For reds, choose a juicy Côtes du Rhône-Villages	Chicken meat is quite delicate, so avoid very assertive wines and go for medium-bodied, well-balanced styles
Chinese/Thai	Off-dry Riesling with Chinese sweet and sour; Gewürztraminer or white beer with aromatic, creamy Thai dishes	Don't touch a red here. Likewise, oaky whites clash. Go for gently acidic, fragrant white wines, and frothy, faintly spicy wheat beers
Chocolate	Australian botrytised Semillon. With chocolate mousse, chilled tawny port	Instant death by chocolate for weedy, light dessert wines. Choose something assertive and rich
Duck	Fruity red burgundy	Duck meat suits sauces made from red berries, and red burgundy is a soft, smooth red redolent of ripe red fruit. It's rather simple, really!
Fish – plain, grilled, white fish fillet	Soft Bordeaux Blanc, Italian Lugana or a fine Soave	Plump for a gentle, but fresh-tasting unoaked white which won't overwhelm delicate fish. Choose one with a lemony flavor, which suits the fish, of course
Lamb – roast	Rioja reserva or gran reserva, or mature claret	Mellow fruit flavors of strawberry and currants work brilliantly, as do smooth rounded tannins and hints of leather or mint

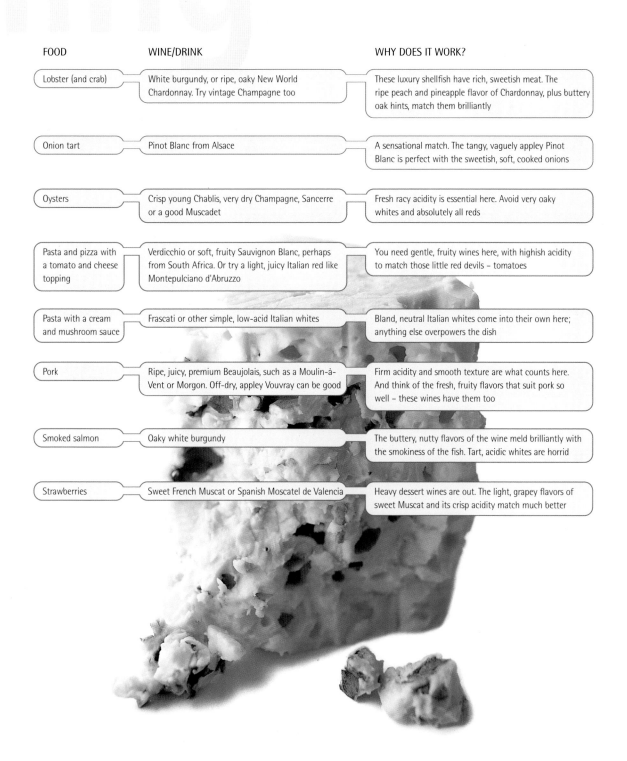

FOOD	WINE/DRINK	WHY DOES IT WORK?
Lobster (and crab)	White burgundy, or ripe, oaky New World Chardonnay. Try vintage Champagne too	These luxury shellfish have rich, sweetish meat. The ripe peach and pineapple flavor of Chardonnay, plus buttery oak hints, match them brilliantly
Onion tart	Pinot Blanc from Alsace	A sensational match. The tangy, vaguely appley Pinot Blanc is perfect with the sweetish, soft, cooked onions
Oysters	Crisp young Chablis, very dry Champagne, Sancerre or a good Muscadet	Fresh racy acidity is essential here. Avoid very oaky whites and absolutely all reds
Pasta and pizza with a tomato and cheese topping	Verdicchio or soft, fruity Sauvignon Blanc, perhaps from South Africa. Or try a light, juicy Italian red like Montepulciano d'Abruzzo	You need gentle, fruity wines here, with highish acidity to match those little red devils – tomatoes
Pasta with a cream and mushroom sauce	Frascati or other simple, low-acid Italian whites	Bland, neutral Italian whites come into their own here; anything else overpowers the dish
Pork	Ripe, juicy, premium Beaujolais, such as a Moulin-à-Vent or Morgon. Off-dry, appley Vouvray can be good	Firm acidity and smooth texture are what counts here. And think of the fresh, fruity flavors that suit pork so well – these wines have them too
Smoked salmon	Oaky white burgundy	The buttery, nutty flavors of the wine meld brilliantly with the smokiness of the fish. Tart, acidic whites are horrid
Strawberries	Sweet French Muscat or Spanish Moscatel de Valencia	Heavy dessert wines are out. The light, grapey flavors of sweet Muscat and its crisp acidity match much better

Index

Acknowledgments

Steve Morris (he took the pic of SA on page 10)
Paul Henry, Enotria Winecellars
Anne Whitehurst, German Wine Information Service
Catherine Manac'h, SOPEXA
Victoria Morrall, Wines of Austria
Ted Bruning, CAMRA
Salva Alfano, Cactus Blue restaurant
R&R Teamwork
Virgin Wines (pics)
Michael Jackson
Jim Beveridge
Neil Cochrane

Nick Morgan
Mike Nicolson, UDV
Vanya Cullen
Henry Butler (for his palate)
Bruce Fraser, for cosmic particle theory,
Jo and Ian, for great ideas at times of crisis
Thanks also to Becca, Jamie, Susan, and the ever-lovely Hils

Dedication: To Boris, Anna, Clara, Daniel & Charlie, the drinkers of
the future.